The
Open
SpACE

Roger Grainger.
RADA 1955

The Open SpACE

ROGER GRAINGER

sussex
ACADEMIC
PRESS

Brighton • Chicago • Toronto

2 4 6 8 10 9 7 5 3 1

First published in 2014 by
SUSSEX ACADEMIC PRESS
PO Box 139
Eastbourne BN24 9BP

and in the United States of America by
SUSSEX ACADEMIC PRESS
Independent Publishers Group
814 N. Franklin Street, Chicago, IL 60610

and in Canada by
SUSSEX ACADEMIC PRESS (CANADA)
1108 / 115 Antibes Drive, Toronto, Ontario M2R 2Y9

British Library Cataloguing in Publication Data
A CIP catalogue record for this book is available from the British Library.

Library of Congress Cataloging-in-Publication Data
Grainger, Roger.
The open space : theatre as opportunity for living / Roger Grainger.
pages   cm
Includes bibliographical references and index.
ISBN 978-1-84519-668-4 (pb : alk. paper)
  1. Theater—Psychological aspects. 2. Theater audiences. I. Title.
PN2049.G68 2014
792.01—dc23

2014012831

Typeset and designed by Sussex Academic Press, Brighton & Eastbourne.
Printed by TJ International, Padstow, Cornwall.
This book is printed on acid-free paper.

CONTENTS

PREFACE BY
SALVO PITRUZZELLA

The theatrical metaphor has been adopted for centuries to describe human life, by virtue of similitude and analogy: life is a 'sort of' stage, people are 'sort of' actors, and there are, more or less hidden, some 'sort of' scripts, to which we cannot but conform.

But what if theatre would be seen as a 'living metaphor' in Paul Ricoeur's sense, which may add a 'spark of sense' in our perception of reality, enlivening our creative appraisal of what we are and what we do? This is Roger Grainger's attempt in this book: he leads the reader in a thorough exploration of the many facets of theatre, to reconsider in a new way some vital aspects of our being in the world and with the others.

He takes into account the different theories of acting and directing, distilling from them some striking notions about human identity and relationships, and showing that it is not just a matter of accepting or refusing the rules of our staged life, but that a principle of freely chosen inter-human communion is implicit in the very nature of theatre.

Seen from this point of view, the theatrical metaphor looses its prescriptive and, ultimately, desperate grip on our self-perception (as in Goffman's analysis of social relationships), and reveals a treasure of unexpected resources.

This revelation occurs because the author is willing to come to terms with his own experience, taking the responsibility to discern theatre that hinders human potentialities from theatre that liberates them. Being an actor himself, the exploration is made from the inside. He recalls with a mixture of passion and wise detachment his first encounter with experimental theatre, and grants the reader with a lively portrait of Joan Littlewood and her entourage.

Preface by Salvo Pitruzzella

In a sense, this book is a *summa* of a lifelong research not only about theatre, ritual and dramatherapy, but about the deep meanings of our lives, a research which Roger Grainger has led with gentle wisdom.

SALVO PITRUZZELLA is Lecturer in Arts Education
at the Fine Arts Academy, Palermo
www.drammacreativo.it

1

THEATRE SPACE

The stage lights go on, the house lights dim: something is starting to happen. We have to find out what it is, and this means we have to wait and see what comes next. Whatever it may be we feel the urge to follow where it leads. Later on, perhaps we may decide to go no further, but not yet. No, not yet!

What we discover is what the play shows us, what it holds out to us for acceptance or rejection, something which cannot be described here and does not really need any description. Certainly the purpose of this book is not to describe theatre, for theatre describes *itself*. All we have to do is allow ourselves to be present. Perhaps, however, there is more than this for us to do. We have, for instance, to move away, wondering where we have been. This is something we do quite easily; indeed we do it very easily indeed because we are so very used to doing it. Only rarely do we wonder why this should be so. Why cling on to something so tenuous, whose actuality is shadowy and, in the light of our human reality, appears misleading or even meretricious?

All the same, this is what we do. This book attempts to spell out the reason why, which means looking at some of the things which happen to us when we take theatre seriously, embracing its presence within our lives as a tool for making sense of ourselves, an experience we should acknowledge as intrinsic to our personhood. There are many ways this can happen, as the theatre itself assumes a whole wardrobe of disguises, but in some way or another it must do so — not only to help us learn about life, but to give us the power to embrace it more wholeheartedly. The purpose here is to look at the subject in the way it sees itself, rather than to analyse it in terms of

1

a model of interpersonal relationship which owes its origin to psychopathology: theatre makes us less neurotic, for instance, by releasing the pressure of feelings which would otherwise be denied expression, sometimes with disastrous results. In fact, Freud[1] himself drew attention to the way in which theatre illustrates this by its actual choice of subject matter, *Oedipus Rex*, *Hamlet* and *Othello* being cases in point, and as Fintan Walsh[2] has pointed out the nexus of ideas involved in psychoanalysis has afforded an explanation of human behaviour and experience to a whole range of playwrights, and still continues to do so.

Theatre and psychotherapy, Walsh says, are "in dialogue" (p. 73) and this has been the case for many years, perhaps even from the time of Aristotle, who describes the effect of a play on its audience as a form of emotional purging[3]. Since then generations of playwrights have recognised the potential of theatre performance for awakening our awareness of emotions which have lain dormant, which in the light of psychoanalytic theory have affected our behaviour in unwelcome ways and had a decidedly negative effect on our personal happiness by making it difficult, or even impossible, to maintain any kind of emotional stability in the way we carry out our lives in the 'real' world. This is the conclusion Walsh himself draws – that theatre and therapy are inevitably connected, fellow travellers even on the road to personal wholeness.

To do this he calls on an extended list of psychotherapists and theatre practitioners who obviously agree with him, ending with a compendium of recognised authorities in both fields who have pointed to a close relationship between theatre and psychological therapies of various kinds – beginning with Evrinov and Iljine, taking in L. Moreno and Fritz Perls, and ending with Sue Jennings and Phil Jones.[4] Thus he manages to encapsulate the contributions made by particular exponents of approaches to healing and wholeness which "centralise the sharing of personal experience" and are themselves "participatory and collaborative", acting as "powerful and emotional holding spaces" (p. 64).

Whereas this is certainly true of theatre, as a final verdict it possesses one serious drawback in holding back from saying how it manages to do this (although most of those mentioned have their own theories about this), or even what it is that is held here, apart from its being done in a way that is "powerful and emotional". Where

Freud saw healing in the release of emotion, Walsh associates it with its containment. Certainly both these things may be true: theatre appears to be able to move in several directions at once. However, like other writers on theatre, Walsh withholds from committing himself on the crucial subject of the fundamental relationship existing between experience and portrayal, of which description itself is only a part – and of which both theatre and therapy are among many alternative expressions. They certainly belong together, but as in every relationship, the reality of their sharing depends on acknowledging the distance which separates them. Both need space in which to be themselves. Theatre is more conscious of this than therapy.

We tend to concentrate on making space *for* drama but it is drama that creates space for us. In his seminal study *The Empty Space*, written in 1968, Peter Brook[5] describes how "a man walks across this empty space whilst someone else is watching him, and this is all that is needed for an act of theatre."

Certainly, providing some kind of space for things to happen is important, for obvious reasons. Nothing will do so otherwise, which is why we use the phrase 'take place' to describe any event at all; and as Brook points out, to concentrate on the setting is to draw attention to its capacity to give birth to some kind of meaningful action; acts and gestures, words and movements which possess the freedom to express themselves, communicating the significance which the space itself confers on them. This is an experience which has been explored in some depth by the gestalt psychologists, who pointed out that it is actually the provision of a recognisable context – a definable shape – that gives meaning to the things we perceive. Context is not all, but it is necessary for anything.

In order to be itself, then, theatre needs space. Space, however, creates theatre. Theatre itself creates space. By making room for itself it gives us room – room in which to expand and to take our own place. The identification of audience member and theatrical personages which Aristotle describes depends on space which is available to be used for this purpose taken up by the imaginative encounter between persons within the space provided for it. The space itself beckons us to such a meeting, and the drama it presents persuades us to go along with it. This is something we do easily and naturally because of our ability to imagine things among and between ourselves and our willingness to share the worlds we imagined.

Unless we are willing to regard the whole of human life in clinical terms, it is hard to see this space-creating human gesture as pathological. Human beings need space in which to form relationships with one another, and the various forms of artistic expression, including theatre, are ways in which they exteriorise this interior movement in order to establish its presence within a shared world. From this point of view theatre is a demonstration of the terms of our well-being, a healthful activity rather than evidence of psychological breakdown. Certainly, as Freud held, it is able to direct a spotlight onto the events and relationships responsible for such breakdowns and is therefore valuable for the purpose of bringing hidden motives to the surface and exposing wounds which have remained unhealed; but this is not all it can do by any means and it would be wrong to concentrate on its usefulness as a tool for psychotherapy at the expense of its intrinsic value within the fabric of human life as the embodiment of our distanced view of the universe of human experience.

For one thing, too intense a concentration on theatre as a medium for psychotherapy – or more accurately, for psychopathological *interpretation* – distorts our appreciation of the sheer scope of theatre as a dimension of human experience, as if we were to say that water were good for washing but only of secondary importance as a way of quenching one's thirst. Perhaps the comparison is not so far-fetched as it may seem; at least, not in a metaphorical sense, for the action of theatre is not to cure, or even diagnose our sickness but to refresh our awareness of life. Once it has achieved this, it is happy to leave the rest to us. Going to the theatre is a renovative experience. If there has been a release of pent-up emotion, so that we feel temporarily drained, we will not complain if we find ourselves able to think and feel more freely and courageously about ourselves and other people when we remember the event, and perhaps find ourselves describing it to other people. We shall probably not regard it as therapeutic, unless we ourselves are psychotherapists; simply as a special kind of freedom – a liberation of the sense of being human, capable of sustaining our identity as a person among persons. We do not feel healed so much as enriched. This is partly due, of course, to the release of psychological tension described by Freud, Perls and Moreno, which has the effect of restoring our psychic balance, so that we leave the theatre as those to whom the world feels subtly different.

The play has given us back to ourselves. It has done this by giving us space to breathe. It is not simply a case of persuading us to transfer our own personal tragedies, comedies and farces onto the backs of a convenient set of fictional characters with whom we find ourselves somehow able to identify; nor is it, as Walsh suggests, a matter of lodging our own feelings within a space we have set aside for the purpose. The space which theatre creates is not for containment but expansion. It is a place for exploration and discovery. Imagination demands freedom to move, opportunity to make new connections; distance to reach across.

This, of course, is the reason for the distance between audience and performer, *theatron* and *skene*, which turns out to be the most important thing about theatre, although some psychological traditions appear to ignore it altogether. Freud regards artistic phenomena as a diversion of sexual instinct which "enables them to be employed for cultural activities of every kind." D. W. Winnicott,[6] certainly, separates the drive from its satisfaction by interposing a 'transitional object' whose purpose is to bridge the gap between the two by being neither, yet participating in both. This manoeuvre depends on imagination as much as it does on libido, enabling unconscious forces to express themselves in ways which individuals may use to reach out to one another across the distance which both divides and defines them. We are defined by the space which separates us and brings us into relation with one another and consequently with ourselves, and distanced by the action of standing back to draw conclusions about what it is that confronts us.

For all this, theatre is not a metaphor, but the process itself in action. The actual presence of theatre guides our choice of language when we try to describe the oscillation of subject and object which characterises our perception of the world surrounding us. We speak of ideas which present themselves to us, positions which people take up, gestures which we and they make, describing episodes in our lives as if they were actual scenes within a play. We set them apart in order to bring them nearer, both to ourselves and the people we are addressing – for the more important the occasion, the more eager we are to find ways of delivering our message as effectively as possible, which will inevitably involve us in a degree of stagecraft so that what is important may stand out in high relief and without the presence of any distractions.

This is one aspect of theatre's ability to show ourselves to ourselves. In plays we can see the way others apart from ourselves dramatise themselves just as we do. This is something they do *in* the play as well as by means of it. Theatre illustrates the way we stand back from whatever it may be that is going on, either to comment on it or simply to see what happens next. Either way, the character in the play creates the space she or he needs in order to make sense of what is happening, just as we in the audience need room to take a broader, more relaxed view of events on stage. We, of course, are more fortunate than they are, protected as we are by an actual visible line of demarcation. Even so the living picture of what being a human being entails embodies the same principle of withdrawal and engagement, exposure and protection set out in the arrangement of audience and acting area and the space between.

This is a principle, not a technique. There are places in which it is asserted apart from theatres, other ways of putting it into practice, not all of them obviously dramatic. Theatre is simply one way of creating the space people need in order to allow themselves to be themselves. Its importance lies in the clarity with which is makes this particular statement. Theatre-space is paradigmatic of the shape of relationship between persons. Apart from any psychotherapeutic properties it may have, in itself it is a celebration of the terms of human existence, the essential nature of personhood. This is the message conveyed by both form and content, a message about ourselves as we are, beings whose life subsists in reaching out to give and receive; reaching across barriers in order to rediscover themselves in the exchange of identities.

Theatre, then, is something we do, rather than something done to us. It is a way in which we exercise our native imagination in order to give substance to an empathic connection with the life of other people which our vulnerability sometimes refuses to recognise. In various ways we play at these encounters with otherness, telling ourselves that they are not actual, so cannot really harm us. By its nature theatre goes out of its way to assure of our safety on this score; so that reassuring ourselves that, after all, 'it's only a game' we allow ourselves to be led deeper and deeper into the experience of sharing to which we owe our humanity. It is something we do. No-one forces us.

Thus, theatre is something we do naturally; characteristically

even. Its many guises constitute a safe place, encouraging us to
venture into regions of our shared world we may hesitate to enter. It
is both special and ordinary – something remarkable which nevertheless remains firmly within our grasp, a way of using imagination
to reinforce our sense of reality. Theatre reminds us that the truths
we live by are always hidden ones – truths which emerge from actions,
and need actions in order to be recognised; thus the embodied feelings and ideas, which give life to imagined scenarios possess a
significance for us which transcends the literal, and we find ourselves
preferring a fabrication which makes sense to an original which so
resolutely refuses to do so, however hard we try . . .

It may be, of course, that we are trying too hard. Perhaps we have
positioned ourselves too close to the thing we are trying to make sense
of: too close to ourselves in fact. Our aim is engagement, a meeting
of selves, not inclusion. Theatre is an invitation rather than an oper-
ation. It uses story to awaken our imagination, but even so it holds
back from addressing us directly, so that when we arrive in the scene
we will do so willingly without feeling manipulated. This, of course,
is how it works, by giving us leave to turn down its offers: space to
decide. If we try over hard to engage, theatre retreats from us, taking
refuge in its nature as fiction. Coleridge's 'willing suspension of
disbelief' lives precisely here – in the space between.[7]

Theatre, then, does not function in space as such but in 'in-
between' space. Actors and audiences, like the play's characters, are
involved in a journey, setting out together in order to arrive somewhere else. Even when the story appears unwilling to permit such a
thing – as for example in *The Cherry Orchard* or *Waiting for Godot* –
the question of endings, final resolutions, home-comings takes up a
major part of the action, as the absence of an ending powerfully
communicates the need for one. Distance conjures encounter even
when it appears boundless: its absence only serves to stimulate imagination and summon up the world this creates for us, a world which
has been given a dimension of reality by the living presence of actors
and audience.

And so we arrive back at the beginning our argument, with the
magnetism of a space which yearns to be inhabited and gives life to
the imaginary creatures who draw us into it, enhancing our own sense
of life through what Jung identified as 'active imagination'.[8] This is
the faculty which is able to translate abstract ideas into personal expe-

riences. Theatre shows us the process by which it happens, presenting us with the reality of a space which is there to be populated, and beckoning ourselves and others into it. Thus theatre gives permission to go forward in this way through its identity as an icon of possibility, or rather, one of *passibility*; the living image of an emptiness open to habitation, a space which is there to be crossed.

Theatre which is aimed at therapy directs attention towards the reassurance given by the fictional identity of the proceedings – the 'safe space' which encourages those entering it to relinquish their defensiveness. Certainly this is something theatre manages to achieve, by erecting a permeable barrier against realities which we find threatening and whose presence seems likely to overwhelm us. Even more important, however, is the reality from which such protection proceeds, the challenge of the empty space and the opportunity we see opening out before us. The need for containment is there, certainly; but without the invitation to move onwards there could not possibly by any kind of theatre at all.

Through its roots in the way human beings perceive the nature of reality, as something open to the creative presence of imagination transforming ideas into events, an understanding of how theatre works must take precedence over theories about its therapeutic applications, even though the two may be closely connected, for no-one would deny that being given leave to take possession of a sense of being more fully alive must promote psychological health, so that it would be foolish to ignore theories based on the defensive importance of aesthetic distance in its function of emotional containment. Nevertheless, single-strand explanations of global experiences rarely succeed in telling the whole story, and a theory in which all the elements are true is a tautology, shutting itself off from any possibility of breaking new ground. To understand theatre it is theatre itself which has to be taken into consideration, not only its effects.

The event is a disclosure which is also a re-discovery. We do much more than simply observe this space. The stage lights go up and we find ourselves somewhere else, somewhere new, but where we have been before. We know what happens in this space because we are part of it; it speaks to us to remind, not instruct, except of course to instruct by reminding. So we find ourselves an actual part of what it is that we are beholding; this is our participation, the life of the play-space in which we find ourselves, along with the actors, embodying a vision which, however many memories it arouses or chords it strikes, was not originally our own but someone else's; someone who, with the willing help of a group of characters and a convenient space, has set out to make it ours.

This space is not only safe and welcoming but also shared. In fact it is both these things because it is shared. It could be said that art itself is rooted in the impulse to share things, not to keep them entirely for oneself. There is nothing impersonal about art, which is always an extreme form of human action emerging from a particular kind of frustration, namely the urgent need to say something which the artist believes cannot be adequately expressed in other more prosaic ways. The urge here is for communication, not simply self-expression; and the matter to be communicated is of a personal nature. Its intimacy invokes an answering sensitivity to ideas and feelings which are not immediately obvious. For the artist, ambiguity is essential; things which cry out to be expressed have, in Emily Dickinson's words, to be "told slant",[9] even to the extent of their outer form appearing to belie an inner meaning. This is not because this has to be deliberately disguised, but it does have to be *protected*, so that its personal nature, in other words its uniqueness, may somehow survive. Using diversionary tactics, art opens us up to hiddenness in a way denied to direct statements calling for straight-forward recognition on our part.

Theatre invites us to join it in a way which is personal and involves accepting its particular mode of existing even before we have any actual knowledge of what this will actually involve us in or have any real idea of what we are being asked to share. With theatre the sharing comes first, simply because nothing at all of a positive nature can happen without it: nothing creative, that is. Actors and audience 'suspend disbelief' together, as the illuminated space signals its own presence and the play reaches out to embrace them. The movement is entirely mutual, wholly shared. It is a fundamental characteristic of theatre, one which stands over against explanations of theatrical experience which concentrate on intra-psychic events. Theatre as communion, shared fulfilment, is in direct contrast with the Freudian notion of catharsis which remains tied to the doctrine of sublimation according to which the urgency of the pleasure principle in individual human beings strives to avoid the charge of narcissism directed at it by a punitive super-ego. One thing seems certain – whatever the indi-

9

vidual experiences on joining the dance of selves within the play-space is difficult to interpret as any kind of psychological manoeuvre in her or his past, but something he or she recognises as a gift bestowed by the presence of others. To put this plainly, it is the space which has been made for us that draws us in; for the space is where others live and move. They do this separately and together, giving us the room to join them. Here before us is the evidence we seek, that proof of our own reality in the eyes of others, lifting us out of ourselves so that others can restore us.

Theatre then is iconic rather than argued. This is a truth of experience, registered through straightforward reflection, so that belief in the unconscious, although a valid hypothesis, is not really necessary in this case. Just as we recognise shapes, movements, sounds, colours without having to think about them, so we recognise drama when embodied in the theatre because we ourselves immediately imagine it in theatrical terms. From this point of view we do not need to explain it, because its job is to explain itself, which it does implicitly, simply by pointing to its own existence. Plays set out to communicate, just as we decide to pay attention to what they may tell us – but the most important thing any play ever says is 'I am a play. Look! I am theatre – and see, this is my space . . . '

2

Play-Space

'I'm riding a bicycle . . . milking a cow . . . painting the house . . .'
Actors play a game in which one of them stands in the middle of a
circle and starts to mime some action or other, which can be anything
they themselves choose but must be plainly recognisable. When
someone asks what it is they are doing, they have to say they are really
doing something else; whereupon the questioner must replace them
in the centre and proceed to mime whatever it was they had claimed
to be doing but clearly weren't. They go on doing this until some-
body else asks them the same question and they answer in the same
way; and so the game continues.

This is a fascinating exercise but not particularly easy to do, which
is why it always gives rise to such hilarity. From the description given
above it appears to be a straightforward list of people's powers of
invention, but it turns out to be considerably more than that. When
you find yourself actually playing it you discover how extremely difficult it is to ignore what you are actually seeing and the more you
concentrate on what you are supposed to be thinking the harder it
becomes to detach yourself from what you are really perceiving – a
fact very well understood by magicians and conjurers of any kind
whatever. The point here however is that this still applies even when
we are ourselves fully aware of what is going on 'in front of your very
eyes'. Certainly these actors know very well what it is that they are
doing here, and so do their audience. Aside from the laughter
prompted by other people's confusion, there is definable satisfaction
to be derived from rising to the perceptual challenge inherent in the
game itself.

Theatre depends on the truthfulness of the image as something

11

able to assert itself even when its authenticity has been consciously denied or even authoritatively countermanded:

> Think when we talk of horses that you see them printing their proud hoofs i' the receiving earth.[10]

Sometimes the image is too vivid, so that it becomes hypnotic. This is more likely to happen when what we are witnessing resonates with presences in our own lives which are psychologically significant but not within our immediate awareness. That is, we are not actually thinking about them at the time, concentrating as we are on what is happening before us; once we do make the connection, however, the symbolism becomes dominant and we are irresistibly drawn into the play's action by the intense personal relevance of what we now discover ourselves to be involved in, so that we are caught up in it to the extent of no longer being able to distinguish ourselves from it. This can happen in any play and to anybody who comes into contact with it, whether they be actors or members of the audience: if the subliminal message has enough personal significance we may fall victim to the pressure it exerts upon our state of mind to follow where the playwright is leading us.

The ability to work at unconscious or semi-conscious levels of human awareness is, of course, a property of all story-telling. We recognise things that have somehow managed to become unfamiliar to us. The story both reminds and reveals; if it resonates powerfully enough the effect can be, as with Strindberg and Genet, a kind of exorcism in which the things we steadfastly refuse to accept about ourselves are wrenched out of us and we are forced to confront them face to face, their presence focused on our awareness with inescapable intensity. Perhaps all playwrights are conscious of the potentially explosive force which lies in their grasp. Sometimes their writing draws particular attention to the process they themselves are engaged in, as in the theatre of Pirandello or, more familiarly perhaps, when Hamlet seizes the opportunity presented by the arrival at court of a group of travelling players:

> ... the play's the thing
> Wherein I'll catch the conscience of the king.[11]

"The conscience of the king." Here theatre is used as a tool within the setting of the play whose intention is broader and less focused. The intention in this case is forensic rather than therapeutic. Christopher Marlowe, however, devotes an entire tragedy to the exposure of forbidden fantasy and the psychologically liberating effect this may have. Gazing on the carnival of presented human pleasures pervaded before him in its undisguised form – the Archetypes of the Seven Deadly Sins, now possessing a reality previously only hinted at and then repressed from consciousness – Faustus can only cry out in rapture. "O, this feeds my soul."[12]

Obviously his catharsis has been specially arranged, contrived by Mephistopheles, whose business is primarily with souls and their manipulation. Released from the power of hiddenness and the need to conceal, Faustus turns gratefully to his benefactor, now revealed as so much more effective a magician than he himself ever was. The conclusions which Marlowe intends us to draw from this concern the depths of impulses of a spiritually destructive nature, and in order to do this they must be shown to be not just ideas but actual presences However destructive as they may be, to expose them in this way is presented as a liberating experience, one which is felt to be psychologically validating; what we choose to do with our new found freedom is another matter.

All the same, to use theatre as a form of expression in such a way is always to stress part of its nature at the expense of the rest of it. The plays in which the authors demonstrate the methods to which their craft may be put are not themselves manipulative in this way. The basic paradigm is present – that of release of tension through imaginative involvement – but the work is always shared, and no-one bullies us into the roles we assume either as actors or members of the audience. It is intrinsic to the nature of theatre as an art form rather than a technique applied to particular situations for the solution of specific problems, that no-one should be constrained to take part against their will, so that it may be nothing less than the free meeting of selves.

At least this is how it should end up being. In fact, however, the experience of taking part in this event is itself very like a play. The course of events leading from the decision to immerse oneself in the play-world from start to finish reproduces the play's own outline as the story of a difficulty overcome, a barrier removed. Plays turn around the image of an impossible possibility, the disaster which, though never averted, is somehow transformed into a triumph. The mixture comes in various strengths, but without it there is no drama worth mentioning and consequently nothing at all to be acted out. (It is worth noting that the barriers in comedy and farce can be just as insurmountable as those in romance and tragedy.) But performing itself, the business of actually doing theatre, is also something of an emotional disaster area.

Obviously the technical difficulties for those whose job it is to devise and direct and perform the play will be considerable, just as audiences themselves have certain arrangements to make in order to be in a position to attend the performance, although these are unlikely to be so difficult or to last so long. The emotional strain is centred upon the difference between two distinct categories of human experience, corresponding to ways of construing reality: two separate 'worlds', in fact, that of observed fact and imaginatively realised fiction, sensed metaphor. As human beings we are familiar with both worlds, although considerably more with the first than the second, and under normal circumstances, we are accustomed to being able to make the transition easily enough, using our imagination to step back and forth whenever we choose to do so.

Theatre, however, is not 'normal circumstances' – far from them in fact. It is to make an issue of something naturally spontaneous, to make public what is private and personal by getting us to share it to a degree we may well find uncomfortably intrusive; to plunge in and 'suspend our disbelief', not only in the scene unfolding around us but in ourselves as balanced, civilised adults with no real emotional diffi-culties of any kind, so that if someone asked us to say how we were getting on, we would almost certainly reply "Very well thank you – and how are you yourself?" These are the folk with whom theatre deals, aiming to make them laugh or cry, or at least ask questions about themselves and their worlds. These are the things which those who labour to create theatre have in mind. They know about them because they, too, are people living in both worlds, and they are aware that something has to be done to bring them together, so that they may be distinguished and related.

This paradigm of a painful encounter is observable in the plot of a play and in the circumstances of its presentation. It is also dramat-ically present in the experience of actors who feel it both as themselves and also in their role as representatives of their fellow travellers in the audience as they break through the barrier between worlds on our behalf. What we are invited to do willingly they carry out in some anguish, as they wait anxiously offstage to make their entrance. This has nothing to do with their acting ability either as professionals or amateurs, but relates to a fear of thresholds themselves, a phenomenon familiar to students of ritual, which theatre focuses effectively, depending as it does on the idea of a transfer of worlds taking place at one specific time and place, or not at all. It is this 'not at all' which so terrifies actors; the awareness that if for some reason they fail to make an entrance the world will stop. In such circumstances, the mind may well go blank, which makes remembering lines almost impossible, yet once on stage they must come to mind easily and naturally as they always have before.[13] The lines, however, belong on stage, to the world of the play; and the actor is trapped in the wings, caught between two conflicting realities.

What they are actually doing, of course, is waiting for the cue to go on stage. When this comes they make their entrance. This is something they do without thinking, triggered into action when the time is ripe and only then. Part of the sequence is not enough; both things go together, the anguished suspense of waiting in the wings and the exhilaration of breathing the air of a world where the sense of life is so much richer, so much more focused. Actors speak of being 'buoyed up' by the concentrated attention of the audience: "Offstage, waiting for the line to come up which is my cue, I'm shaking with terror. Then I go on and it's as if a tide of feeling is there to welcome me, coming up towards me from the audience." I asked this actor what he meant by 'feeling'. I don't know, he said, "it's almost a kind of warmth."[14]

This actor is one of the many to whom I have spoken over the years, usually on the subject of 'stage fright'.[15] The term refers specifically to the fear of *going* into the acting area and not of *being* in it. It is a subject close to an actor's heart, which comes up with alarming frequency when actors talk about their craft. Students of theatre itself, it appears, rarely mention the subject. However, it is of immense importance for any understanding of how theatre functions and what it stands for in the economy of human experience. From this point of view, stage fright is paradigmatic of theatre itself. If drama concerns conflict, here it is, at the very heart of the entire process; if it embodies

15

the experience of shared selfhood and all that this implies in terms of human sorrow and joy, then an actor's terror and restoration are more significant for the way the play itself works than she or he realises.

We should not be surprised that the actor's experience is an extreme one. After all he or she operates right at the epicentre of the theatrical happening. They don't stand there alone, for they carry the audience with them. This is their function. Anything we feel or think about the play, we the audience do in and through the actor who impersonates us – not only by being a member of the same species as ourselves, but because she or he is someone with whom we are able, if we choose, to identify in ways which may be profound but are always personal.

That is, we can do so if we choose; if, that is, we are willing to allow ourselves to become so involved in the play's action as to feel and think our own versions of the emotional experiences of its characters – or of a particular character whose situation, as acted out before us, has caught our attention and awakened our own emotional memory. This will not depend wholly on the actor's skill in conveying the inner life of his or her character, any more than the audience's determination to regard what is going on in the play as applying directly to themselves. As we saw to begin with, it will always involve the willingness on both parts to collaborate in the creation of imagination *for its own sake*. Theatre liberates our emotions in a way which we find acceptable and are willing to co-operate with. In some cases the release of emotion has clinical significance; but as we saw earlier, this cathartic function of theatre is by no means the only thing which gives it the special value it has for us. In fact its ability to relieve psychological pressure is a result of a much more fundamental property which theatre possesses – that of validating human relationship across the barriers which separate and define us.

This is not a matter of containing emotion but of allowing it to be released in a way which is positive and life-enhancing, turned outward toward the other person rather than inwards towards oneself and one's own private world. Theatre is feeling 'outside the box', in which we use the play and our own participation in it as an excuse for abandoning our customary caution in regard to letting ourselves to be known as we really feel ourselves to be. Taking advantage of the opportunity to assume a new identity offered by the play itself, along with the terms of our involvement in it, we find ourselves leaving one role – the one role we have played outside the theatre – aside, so that we can now take possession of a completely different one. Certainly this new identity as a 'citizen of the theatre' promises to involve us in things we have largely forgotten; overall, however, the exchange is felt to have been worthwhile: we feel more in touch with ourselves and closer to each other. Or rather, to one another, for this relationship is felt to be essentially transpersonal, a sharing in which our need for exclusiveness, the hold we have on our privacy has somehow been loosened.

It has not simply come loose, however, as if magically unravelled by the power of theatre. We co-operate with what is happening to us because we really want it to happen. We need both to escape from ourselves and to join up with others; at the same time, however, we must do so carrying ourselves with us, not leaving anything behind which we feel is essential or at least very important to us. Up to now we have worked on the assumption that our security lay in preserving at least part of ourselves as sacrosanct, a place to which no-one else is allowed entrance. This, we tell ourselves, is the real truth about myself. It is, in fact, the real *me*. It would be easy to see this attitude of mind as a kind of illness, as indeed, in its extreme form, it may become pathological. It is not only psychologically ill people who make this assumption, however; it comes so easily to us that it doesn't even need thinking about. We simply take it for granted that when it comes down to it, we belong only to ourselves.

Theatre, however, is founded upon a different premise. In it we set about relinquishing privacy – our privacy – for acceptance, and benefiting from the exchange. Accepting the challenge of moving imaginatively into the life of someone else involves abandoning the false security of refusing to do so, a situation familiar to us at every stage of our lives. We are accustomed to think that the choice is entirely optional and that no-one else is in a position to require us to take this risk. Nor, for that matter is theatre, which refuses to work its magic without our willing co-operation; which in fact cannot do so unless we freely agree to help – once the apprentices decide to leave the sorcerer is rendered powerless. In *The Tempest* it is the island itself which casts its reconciling spell, consummated in the union of Ferdinand and Miranda: once this is accomplished, then Prospero drowns his book.

In theatre we do not just agree, we co-operate. The play will not simply happen, but must be willed into being. This action of co-creation is the fulcrum on which theatre rests, the point on which it turns. The surrender of our customary autonomy regarding the things we ourselves decide to feel and think is brought directly into focus here as nowhere else. This isn't an actor's game, nor a playwright's either, but a serious decision on our parts to put ourselves emotionally in others' hands and be willing to suffer the consequences. It requires not just willingness but an act of will.

One we are used to making. We have grown used to it and largely forgotten how necessary it is. We are reminded, however, when, having taken our seats, we wait for the play to begin . . . Then we too have our own version of stage fright; then we may be conscious of the spectre haunting times such as these, the 'liminal terror' which affects those entering upon initiation into a privileged condition, a new way of being that is at one and the same time both liberating and arduous.[16] We, of course, have been here before, but that appears to make little difference; in fact it may make matters worse, because this particular nervousness is really something we expect. It is a necessary part of going to the theatre. We would not enjoy a play so much without it.

"I don't know why," an actor says, "but unless I'm scared before I go on, it never seems to go well. Somehow I find it hard to get into the play."[17] Theatre is not about dispensing with barriers but finding the way to tackle them. The rule applies both on and offstage. To imagine a situation is quite easy: we do it all the time, usually without having to try; but to regard an imaginary world as if it were real enough to take seriously and become emotionally involved in calls for a particular use of imagination, one which requires it to come boldly out into the open and allow itself to be recognised, so that by collaborating with others it may be put to good use for the construction of a fictional alternative universe.

If this fails to happen then there is no play, only disappointment and a good deal of resentment on everybody's part. Certainly we have all known occasions when this has been the case. We are angry because we feel frustrated, having prepared ourselves for our imaginary journey and find ourselves somehow thwarted; but in fact the first stage is already achieved.

3

ANGRY SPACE

> We expect to enjoy ourselves at the theatre and are annoyed unless, in someway or other, we do. After all, we go because we like to play with our imaginations and gain satisfaction and emotional release from so doing. If people don't they get cross and walk out. I've even known actors do this, in fact. In theatre, if you don't join in you've no chance of getting anything out of it. Instead of being bored, you just get very angry.

This is part of a letter from an actor who has asked to remain anonymous. I have quoted it here because it underlines a characteristic of theatre which, although some are delighted by it, certainly causes embarrassment to many others. Those who are annoyed and disconcerted usually demand that theatre should never really be taken too seriously. Make-believe, they point out, should not be allowed to give offence, certainly not cause distress. A play, they say, is after all only a play . . . and those responsible for theatre should not be permitted to forget the fact.

On the other hand theatre which is awkwardly, or sometimes disconcertingly, emotionally disruptive causes a degree of satisfaction to anyone keen to recognise signs of mental breakdown. This attitude draws its justification from the psychoanalytic tradition, and indeed, as noted in Chapter 1, from Freud himself. Many psychologists and psychotherapists regard theatre as a way of relieving the pressure of feelings which threaten to disturb our mental balance. The violence embodied in theatre acts as an emetic, ridding the system of impulses which have become all the more dangerous through being hidden. Aristotle's vision of an imagination purified by our identification

19

with others' suffering is medicalised into a method of overcoming all the strengths of our passions simply by inducing us to 'let off steam', as if it were the power to feel, to take things seriously and apply them to oneself which lay at the root of the problem.

Theatre itself may go out of its way either to bully us or protect us from feeling we have to get in any way involved. All the same, emotion is its subject matter and its principal purpose is to display it; it fails, therefore, whenever it is unable to get its message across. The communication takes place 'between feeling and feeling', however the intellect chooses to interpret it. This is true of all plays, however light-hearted and apparently trivial they may actually claim to be. We may assume a consciously detached attitude towards what- ever is happening on stage, but for the characters in the play these things are of the greatest importance; to those of us who are in a posi- tion, as members of the audience, to take the broader view, what appears scarcely worth bothering oneself about is to the people in the play a matter of immediate concern. We may remain aloof, but they cannot possibly do so.

Whatever theatrical genre it may belong to, the story deals with things which cause its characters distress. Its crux is always some- thing regarded as both necessary and impossible. For the characters themselves, the situation is dominated by their fear of failure, of being defeated in whatever it may be that they have set their minds on carrying out, whether this is the achievement of some ambitious project, or simply managing to get to the post office before it closes. The story's climax arrives when events make it unavoidably obvious that such a thing can now never happen; and it is the emotional impact of this that gives the story its shape: that in fact makes it a story at all. Without the arousal of a reaction which the character involved feels immediately disempowering, there can be no real reso- lution of the crisis – no outcome, whether tragic, comic or simply reassuring, with things 'turning out all right in the end'.

Whether tragic or comic, theatre concerns actions impelled by feelings. This is intrinsic to the scenario itself, as both the form and content of what is being displayed transmit action originating in and driven by emotion. As Aristotle first pointed out, "the plot is the soul of the drama"[18] through its ability to engage us at a level of aware- ness preceding rational judgement. Thus theatre is a convenient tool or even a powerful weapon in the hands of those whose purpose is to manipulate our thoughts in a direction which they themselves have chosen. In fact, as we saw in Chapter 1, this fundamental emotionality of theatre is able to overcome our conscious attempts to defeat it by stressing the wholly fictional nature of the events being acted out in our presence. Remember, we say, this is only a play; and the more we say it the less we question its truthfulness. It is not theatrical realism which causes us to 'suspend disbelief'[19] but the play's way of reminding us of things about ourselves which we know to be true.

It is realism rooted in feelings. We respond to emotions expressed and embodied by the people within the play and recognised as authentically present in ourselves also. It is this unquestioned sharing of experience which seals drama as inalienable human truth, when understanding itself clings to the evidence presented by our perception of a world which withholds meaning from us. Left to themselves the phenomena we perceive preserve their anonymity, refusing to have any life for us unless we show willingness to bestow it on them – or rather, to exchange it with them. We believe in what we feel to be the case; only then do we set about convincing ourselves that we are being reasonable.

Unfortunately we are well able to argue ourselves out of immediate reach of feelings which for one reason or another cause us discomfort or inconvenience. In psychological terms we repress them into unconsciousness or train ourselves to deny their power to trouble our minds. Antonin Artaud felt passionately about theatre's potential ability to destroy our inhibitions about acknowledging the reality of the turbulence within ourselves. He advocated a theatre able to engage our feelings to such a degree that the intellect would be forced to relinquish its hold over the emotional life of civilisation which has taught itself to discount anything about humanness save its ability to argue. "Abandoning psychology," he says, "theatre must narrate the unusual, stage nature's conflicts, nature's subtle powers . . . This is where theatre, far from imitating life, communicates wherever it can with pure forces."[20]

Artaud is campaigning against plays which set out to demonstrate psychological theories about human motivation. His rage is directed against them because they blaspheme theatre's real purpose, which both on and offstage must primarily be to promote the release of feeling on behalf of society itself, not simply to provide therapy for individuals. His 'cruelty' involves all present, whether on stage or in

the audience: all are involved in situations of violence and depriva-
tion extreme enough to weld together actor and spectator, sweeping
both along in an irresistible tide of passion across the division which
is there to keep them safely apart from one another, treating it as the
symbol of restraints which inhibit, barriers that must be broken down
in order for life itself to flourish.

Artaud's view of theatre may seem extreme, and in fact it has never
really been put to the test. Its main importance lies in its usefulness
as an inspiration for those who find themselves disenchanted with
theatre which hesitates to involve its audience in what is going on at
anything but the shallowest kevel. For all those for whom theatre is
itself a passion, much of what passes in the commercial world for
theatre is both boring and frustrating. Many who work in theatre
regard it as a vocation rather than a profession, even though they
probably feel self-conscious if you ask them about it. Inspired by an
experience of theatre which they themselves found irresistible, they
carry with them the vision of a source of emotional fulfilment which
is, or should be, available to everyone if they are willing to surrender
to its force.

Such then, in a milder, more civilised form, is the legacy of
Antonin Artaud, expressed as the urge for a depth of emotional life
of which daily existence is starved and for which at one level of awareness we are yearning to share with one another. This is what Charles
Williams referred to as "the unstinting nature of man"[21] which is
enlarged by feeling rather than thought; or rather by thought which
emerges from feeling in order to nourish it. Theatre is active emotion
in the form of embodied imagination; what happens to us in our
imagination belongs to our own personal reality to the extent that we
relate it to our own truth and by embodying it in action make it part
of ourselves. In this way imagination actualises emotions, making
them, in Jung's term, "active".[22]

In its embodied form emotion establishes its own truth with an
authority it would otherwise surely lack. Indeed, it is almost impossible to conceive of it in any other way, as detached emotion is a
contradiction in terms. It is what happens to living human beings,
rather than abstractions, that moves us, as in imagination we translate their flesh into our own and our own into theirs. This is what
Williams means when he writes of times "when emotion is full,
strong and efficient".[23] These are occasions when we are brought into

contact with parts of our own nature of whose presence and significance we were unaware – feelings which we never felt before or have tried hard not to feel.

These unexplored selves are brought to light by the play's invitation to immerse ourselves in its action, by giving ourselves permission to allow the life of embodied imagination to enrich our own reality. Thus the play moves from life to life, borne along by the emotions it revives in those taking part, whether they be actors or audience. This is the unifying power which transforms a difference – a distance – into a wholeness, as shared emotion finds expression by leaping the gap. Martin Buber's experience of theatre's power to do this inspired an entire lifetime of exploring human truth as "betweenness",[24] by which he means the life which springs forth in the meeting of persons, not disembodied ideas.

Even though we may not actually touch one another, the scenario binds us together in ways which are authentically personal, interrupting our preoccupation with our own concerns and turning us, at least for the time being, toward the other. The emotion we feel originates with ourselves, our own past and present experiences, but its object is someone else, or perhaps a group of other people; and we do not merely transfer feeling to them, we exchange it with them. Here in the theatre we are co-inheritors of one another's emotions. The principle remains the same whether the emotion involved is august or derisory, evoked by a profound truth concerning the human condition, or trivial and commonplace – embarrassment, frustration, boredom, straightforward annoyance. It is not only our own reaction but others' as well, and they ours, and it takes place at an emotional level, not a cognitive one.

In other words, we are not aware at the time that these feelings are not entirely our own, or for that matter, that they may not even be ones we are accustomed to having in any case. This comes later, as we reflect on the time we spent in the theatre, on the distinctive atmosphere of unselfconscious comradeship which we associate with the experience of taking part in a theatrical event: "I felt we were all in it together." If we try to explain this we run the risk of destroying it altogether, as so often happens with psychological procedures. Individual human experience always defies analysis, so much more the interpersonal sharing of experience. Effects may be noted, but the reasons for them remain metaphysical rather than scientific.

All the same, theatre leads us nearer to the heart of the mystery by bringing home the close affinity between feeling and imagination – by actually embodying it in actions which involve us in the process of demonstrating it. Described sequentially, what happens is this: the actor's imagination addresses the imagination of the member of the audience; which sends back its own message in confirmation of the one received; drawn by its intimate association with imagination and memory, feeling follows an identical path; because imagination searches out for scenarios, the play emerges, brought to life by the emotions invested in it which now find a common lodging-place where their individual reality can be strengthened and established by the presence of others.

Compared with the actual experience of being present for even a single act of *The Cherry Orchard*, trying to describe theatre like this seems a pointless exercise. Chekov's creation and our participation – what we have all been involved in creating together – says more to us about theatre itself than any attempt to analyse it – even one which manages to be more subtle than the one I am suggesting here. One thing is sure, however, which is that actor and audience engage with each other in the imaginary passions of the stage character. The characters themselves are fictions, the work of imagination, possessing neither passion nor life; they are brought alive by the passions lodged in them by those whose imaginations they set in motion. Actors possess imagination and so do audiences. The same is not necessarily so with the characters imagined by playwrights. Unlike Hamlet himself, Horatio has no "mind's eye"; he, however, does not need to stand back from this as his friend does and can simply get on with whatever is going on in the play itself, whereas Hamlet communicates with us by speaking his troubled mind aloud. In his imagination, Shakespeare's and the audience's meet, and the effect is unforgettable.

Hamlet has no doubt of the power of an imaginary passion to affect reality, as with the help of the players he arranges for his uncle the King to be "frighted with false fire" (Act III sc. 2). The play arouses feelings in Claudius which are powerful enough to force him to reject the play as whole-heartedly as those who walk out of theatres always do. His reasons are certainly more pressing than theirs, but all such occasions demonstrate the robust association which exists being imagination and emotion which theatre epitomises. We look for an enjoyable release from having to think too much, and instead find ourselves "frighted with false fire". It will, of course, be better to stay even if this involves our getting burned; and in fact it may well be that it is when there appears to be no possibility of our being even slightly singed that we finally decide to walk out of the theatre.

At every stage of the theatre process feeling leads the way through the work of imagination: in conceiving the dramatic situation, identifying the characters involved, finding a director, choosing the actors; then designing the setting, including lighting and sound; next, learning lines and starting to move into character while bringing the play to life in rehearsal. All this, even up to the business of advertising and publicity, is the work of the emotional imagination, active within the creative process as it is expressed through author, actor, director, designer, musicians, lighting expert, make-up artist, wardrobe mistress, stage manager and his or her assistants, all in fact who have a role within the theatre. This, of course, includes that of being a member of the audience — which turns out to be the most important role of all.

4

REMEMBERED SPACE

The role of audience member involves not only being present at the performance and finding oneself somehow included in the action, but also, and just as importantly, reflecting on the experience afterwards. This is something which belongs specifically to audiences and should not be confused with actors' and directors' reminiscences, which can hardly avoid being affected by their opinions regarding their own individual contribution to the proceedings. The member of an audience, however, possesses a greater degree of objectivity, not having been in contact with the play for so long a time or with so much effort and determination.

Which makes it all the more remarkable that the memory of a single evening spent at the theatre should remain so clear for so long. Perhaps the actor whom I quoted earlier will forgive me if I include the following, taken from further on in the same letter:

> Last month I went to see _____, who is now, as I'm sure you know, living in a care home in the village where I used to live myself. The poor man is crippled with arthritis (which is why he's there, having no relatives). For some reason he was eager to talk about a play he saw sometime in the 1950s. He couldn't remember what the play was called and only vaguely knew what it was about, 'but I've never forgotten it, and I don't think I ever will'. That was the reason he told me about it – he'd never forgotten it, you see.

It may well be, of course, that he had only been rarely to the theatre, so that when he did go, it made more of an impression on him than it would have done on a regular theatre-goer; but even if this were the case, the experience of 'never forgetting' a play is exceedingly well documented, as also the difficulty in remembering exactly what happened in it, not so far as the actual details of the plot are concerned. What is remembered is the emotional impact which, after all this time, manages to persist in having its effect on our state of mind. The impression is intense yet indeterminate, a unique way of remembering that works subliminally within awareness, as the after-image of a revelation which resists our efforts to tie it down. We know that it happened in a play; we may even remember which one it was; but how and why it happened we can never be certain.

We remember plays because of times like this. The scenario carries us along with it, but the meaning of the whole arrives as an unannounced moment of discovery, a cognitive-emotional breakthrough. This, we say, is what the play was about, so that it may not really matter if it turns out to be all we remember of it. This, for us, *was* the play, the one we will never forget . . . Plays use stories in order to set the scene for a particularly vivid kind of emotional event, characterised by Sartre as "the moment of truth".[25] This is the juncture at which things which have been disturbingly out of alignment suddenly fall together into place. In terms of the story, this announces a new state of affairs which may be either better or worse for those involved, but because it comes as a shock, manages to lock itself into our emotional memory.

Theatre's ability to encapsulate emotional experience is an important aspect of the way it works, which is more by impression than argument. We do not follow the narrative to find out where events are leading so that we too can reach a conclusion regarding our own subsequent path through life. At least, this is not what we consciously set out to do, although this may well turn out to be the end result as we reflect upon the play as a whole.

This, however, is something we do later on. Now, at this time, the whole is what we are experiencing and we ourselves are part of it; which is why, when we do come to look back, it is the experience itself which we remember rather than any attempts at analysis. We recall the sense of the play as it was brought to life for us by the moment or moments when we ourselves engaged with it and it brought us to life. These are the occasions we recall when we think of the play. They are the times when it became our own story, registering itself as an authentic event in our life, capable of

27

functioning as a moment of decision, a genuine turning-point for us.

In such a way as this an experience becomes an idea, choosing as midwife a significant life-event. Because of the emotional intensity of the encounters it frames for us, theatre certainly qualifies as such an event, a staging post in the way we construct our meanings. This then is the most important gift made by theatre to human under-standing, a way in which we are helped to make sense of what we feel. Things felt in theatre give rise to theories about theatre, as the present book itself demonstrates. However theatre itself as a human phenom-enon is not simply a way of thinking about things; it certainly makes use of texts but is not one itself. It's connection with our sense of being alive is closer. The actor whom I quoted earlier, speaking of a particularly vivid experience of her own, told me "I don't know if it really happened to me or if it was in a play I once saw."

Michel Foucault describes how, in its raw state theatre concerns happenings rather than ideas, thoughts, theories *about* events, all of which are ways in which we attempt to discount the distance sepa-rating perception itself from whatever it is that is being perceived. This 'difference' is something which, left to ourselves, we deal with by containing it within a conceptual framework in which it "is trans-formed into what must be specified within a context without over-stepping its limit."[26] What Buber described as "the stern over-againstness"[27] of theatre presents us with events which refuse to allow us to take them over in such a way, thus retaining their own life while invigorating – enlivening – ours.

Foucault, like Artaud, proclaims the play's truthfulness regarding people's need for experience which is authentically other-directed, and interrupts the process by which we attempt to forestall events by understanding them in advance. He draws attention to

the privileged stage ... multiplied, polyscenic, simultaneous, broken into separate scenes that refer to each other and where we encounter without any trace of representation (copying or emulating) the dance of masks, the cries of bodies and the gesturing of hands and fingers.[28]

In other words, a completely different worldview from our usual one, having been activated by the interruption of the one we are so very familiar with and automatically take for granted.

This is theatre as perceptual re-investigation. Thought and feeling are surprised into life and the creative relationship between them renewed. Theatre chimes with human existence because the language it uses is the experience of invigorated awareness. The thrice-told story uses a range of approaches: organic, structural and linguistic. First of all there is the level of perceptual function, then that of the dramatic ordering of the play's events, and lastly, the spoken and performed record of human journeying and arrival; in other words what the characters say the play is actually about. In these three ways the message is brought home as something more than a striking piece of information to be accepted or rejected in a way that is strictly reasonable. The play is not just data but something which is actually happening to us.

So we find ourselves returning to the main theme of this study in which the question is asked, Why Theatre? What is so special about it? As we saw to begin with, it is a way of making space in life, of pausing to change the subject; of giving ourselves permission to take time off from ourselves and our immediate preoccupation with the task of concealing our own vulnerability; a space for allowing ourselves to feel our own and others' pain by loosening our grip, at least temporarily, on trying so hard not to have to do so – in other words of allowing ourselves to belong more wholeheartedly within the company of others and so celebrate a common humanity.

In theatre we make room for feeling by giving body to thought. Theatre turns memory and reflection into immediacy. There is no space for such things because it has been taken up by people – *these* people. We may explain this by telling ourselves that, in them, we recognise our own condition; in fact, however, we simply recognise them as people, embodied presences, welcoming us to share their world with them. It is the welcome which we recognise, because this is what we are looking for, the validation which comes from people, not simply ideas but human beings like ourselves. Theatre facilitates the encounter of persons. For cultures which depend on information technology to the extent of our own, its role is obviously extremely important, perhaps even essential, underlining the significance of a crucial difference between the transmission of data regarding people and the experience of meeting them 'in the flesh'.

This it is that sticks in the memory. It does so as event not infor-mation; the feeling enshrined in a particular occasion, which memory shows itself capable of bringing to the surface even when we have forgotten what it was that actually happened, and find difficulty in describing it to anyone else. This is not at all surprising. After all, what happened was between ourselves and the other people who were there at the time. This can be frustrating; after all it is the actual experience which still cries out to be shared with others, and this is actually something which can never be adequately described except in terms of the feelings which it arouses. Far from describing events, theatre effectively brings home the limits of description. Certainly, if we use our memory efficiently – as we have been trained to use it – we can remember the plots of plays which we have seen, and this may turn out to be necessary if we want to arrive at considered judgements about them; but what concerns us most is not the story itself but what happened in it. What, in fact, happened to *us* in it.

The story is a good one if something happens to us in it: if we let something happen to us. We speak in terms of a story 'getting through' to us, but of course we ourselves have to be willing to allow such a thing to happen. Storytellers announce their entry into a fictional world, signalling us to follow. Whether we decide to do so depends on their skill in 'setting the scene'. In theatre, of course, scene-setting is not only verbal. The provisional nature of the enterprise is communicated architecturally, by buildings dedicated to the purpose, and we have pledged our willingness to participate by paying to go in. Going to see a play is demonstrably more of an event than listening to a story. There is little doubt that we know what we are doing and the nature of the decision we have taken.

If the ability to see the play as something in which we ourselves are personally involved depends upon our own willingness to allow it to happen, then the action of going to the theatre is extremely significant. As the event embraces us, so we embrace it. Story and presentation, time and place, interact here as they do in life, so that the occasion establishes itself as lived experience prior to any conclusions we may draw from it. Of course, we are bound to look for reasons why it impressed us so strongly, and some of them will involve retracing the journey we made through the plot's successive stages in order to rediscover what it was that touched us so very personally. Aristotle refers to plot as "the soul of the drama". Souls are not minds, they leave analysis to the intellect, while they themselves respond to life in ways which are unguessable. As far as theatre goes, the plot provides the opportunity for what happens among and between people. The elderly care home resident could no longer say what it was that happened, only that it did and was worth remembering – that it still managed to live on even when its story had been largely forgotten.

Thus theatre, in its effects upon the way we perceive life and the world around us, has an iconic quality, communicating a wholeness which refuses to be spelled out, the speaking outline of a transformative understanding, the image of an inhabitable mystery. This is something which clings to the medium itself and is therefore able to affect the meaning of everything brought into contact with it, so that what would otherwise be trivial becomes, in theatre's hands, significant or at least important enough to be taken seriously – by the heart if not always the mind, which will have its own opportunities later on.

The question as to which is most important for theatre, mind or heart, is a familiar one, having been asked many times by generations of writers since Aristotle himself. His answer is one which suggests that both are equally important, but that it is the heart which leads the mind. We might add that, so far as the play itself goes and the experience of being involved in it, the heart sets the pace; not only when the play being watched deals with great events involving famous people, but equally when the opposite is true. Audiences identify with clowns as readily as they do with princes. This does not mean that they do so uncritically, at least to begin with, but that once the heart itself has been touched criticism is suspended, put on hold until a more balanced view of events presents itself for consideration.

Whatever it was about the play which the actor's friend remembered so fondly concerned the heart more than the mind, an example of affect triumphing over cognition. All the same, it was a memory of an actual play, a real visit to the theatre which reactivated the feeling of something wholly specific, an emotional excitement focused on a particular moment within the play which could now be recaptured as a living experience, which in fact it still was. In an enduring way, theatre integrates our relationship to the world with our own personal first-hand knowledge of it. We are not just to be reminded about life, as if the play's main purpose were simply to explain us to ourselves. On the contrary, we ourselves are the ones actually doing the explaining. In our involvement with the life of the characters we are occupied in solving problems which belong to life both inside and outside the theatre-space.

If theatre teaches us anything, it is that involvement with life is precisely what we are looking for. In a way, this is something we already suspected, hence our decision to come to the theatre in the first place. We came hoping that somehow or other we might get involved. The release we seek is from the burden we impose on ourselves through our decision to go our own way, follow our private path, ignoring any impulse to reach out to others either for receiving or giving; to use a time-honoured phrase, we "don't want to be beholden". It is a frame of mind which we associate with enjoying ourselves, 'having a good time' or even 'looking after ourselves', implying that given the chance, others will somehow want to stop us doing this. At such times we may well think of visiting the theatre in order to relax and be entertained.

Theatre is certainly able to relax us, but it does so at a deeper level than the word 'entertainment' suggests. What is made less rigid is our defensiveness: the determination we have to maintain a close watch on ourselves in case we reveal too much of whatever it may be that we would prefer to keep to ourselves. In such circumstances the expression of emotion can be dangerous, even among friends. Theatre definitely makes this easier for us, as we are reassured by the fictional nature of the proceedings that nothing thought or felt here need count against us in the real world. All the same the experience of perceiving at this level of intensity registers itself as both real and important. As we have just seen, this is an experience which leaves its mark.

So we are looking for something and find something different. Instead of amusement we discover involvement. This is something we were not really looking for, and the surprise of finding it may be one of the reasons why it sticks in our memory more certainly than it would have done if we had set out to unearth something of real value regarding ourselves. Actually it may turn out that this is precisely what has in fact happened to us; but it wasn't what we were expecting and took some time to sink in.

5

OCCUPIED SPACE

One man in his life plays many parts.
As You Like It, Act V

Shakespeare's Jacques summarises the various stages in a human life-time, each of which involves the person concerned in playing a different but clearly distinguishable social role. From this point of view, role stands for other people's expectations concerning a person's attitudes and behaviour, which should conform to a pattern considered appropriate for his or her age, abilities and social standing. Jacques points to the most obvious examples of role-apportionment, those governed by age. All human roles constitute a limit to the scope of human freedom, those imposed by age being the most strikingly dramatic, because in fact they are the least flexible.

Life, Jacques suggests, imitates theatre. He is able to do so, and we to agree with him, because the reverse is assumed to be true, that theatre imitates life. All the same, we are entitled to ask if this is actually the case, and if so, in what way and to what extent? Is life actually so dramatic? Robert Landy, a distinguished dramatherapist, has drawn up a taxonomy of social and interpersonal roles based on fictional individuals, characters occurring in plays throughout the world,[29] while the concordance which holds between ways of 'staging' social encounters and the presentation of drama in the theatre or by electronic means has been recognised by a generation of sociologists and social psychologists from Erving Goffman onwards. Explicit in theatre, cinema, television and radio, drama never ceases to be implicit within ordinary life.[30] None of this proves, however, that this everyday drama is really very like

33

theatre, however hard we try to make a case for arguing that such is the case.

The most that can be said is that in order to approximate a dramatic effect it makes use of some of the basic structures of theatre, such as hero-as-opposed-to-villain, wise-person-as-opposed-to-fool, backstage-as-opposed-to-fore-stage. Whether these strategies were first learned within a fictional scenario, as for instance a children's game, or whether they should really be seen as a characteristic of the human species, exploited for purposes of instruction and entertainment is not the main issue. They are used for the purpose of what Goffman refers to as "impression management", and there is no real excuse for supposing that the impression we are meant to receive is that of an actual piece of theatre. They are rhetorical devices and we are not taken in by them.

There is more to theatre than the use of dramatic conventions. Theatre does not set out merely to imitate life even though its characteristic ways of presenting dramatic situations appear so life-like. Drama's intention is to draw attention to the stratagems we use to achieve our ends rather than using them against us, not to teach us roles to play but to expose our own role-playing for what it is. Theatre's aim is never merely to reproduce human behaviour but to affect it. This is why it is so careful to choose the examples of behaviour it brings to our attention; for even the most realistic description of a course of events leaves out details which the narrator considers irrelevant. If theatre imitates life it does so with discretion.

There is not much difference, then, between the way we learn social roles and theatrical ones; from this point of view the stage is like the world, the locus of perceived experience. It is the quality of the experience, however, which makes all the difference. Despite the realism imported by memory and imagination, theatre distorts our normal perception of events by presenting reality in ways which are both *selective* and *heightened*. Again, these are interactive effects rather than separate ones, as the author's choice of episodes to make up the story intensifies its emotional impact and directs us to a central core of meaning, as feeling and thought spring to life through our own developing relationship with the play's characters.

As we saw in the last chapter, it is these moments which we remember because they are the ones which impact most upon our awareness, affecting our own experience of ourselves and our world.

34

This is not because we make a considered decision to mould ourselves on a particular stage character, adopting his or her role as our own (this may happen sometimes, of course, but probably not very often), but in a much less formal and stereotyped way, powerful but also impressionistic, characterised by the process identified by Piaget as 'accommodation' rather than 'assimilation'. In other words the play adapts itself to our own readiness to receive it, instead of providing us with a convenient role model, something we can decide to accept or reject according to whether it suits us. Our personal lives may well reflect some of the plays we have absorbed into ourselves, but not because we set out with the intention of making this happen.

Jacques, however, is a character played by an actor, and it is certainly an actor's job to take on roles. For actors, the world is populated by characters rather than people – although not impersonal ones, because it is the personality of a character that an actor aims at assuming. In this sense it is true that for them at least "all the world's a stage"; and actors at social gatherings look at their fellow guests with a strictly professional eye, storing up details of facial expression, posture, tone of voice, all recorded for future use in the task of role-creation.

It is not only other people that actors scrutinise, however. They also look at themselves for inspiration. Peter Hall used to remind members of his cast that whatever role they were attempting these would always be something at hand within their own personality able to come to their aid.[31] It is this that gives life to the character being played, combining authenticity with imagination, because it is always the voice of experience, of someone able to communicate at first hand with a passion which is genuine. It is certainly true what Jacques has to say about "playing many parts". What he omits saying, however, is that many of them are played concurrently, such as when the same individual manages to function successfully in more than one role-relationship, as for instance those of husband/father, teacher/learner, actor/audience member.

In fact it is usual to play several roles in life, some of which in other circumstances would certainly contradict one another, and to do so entirely sincerely, or even whole-heartedly. The action of assuming a role is not to be seen as indicative of a desire to deceive. Roles are not masks, and in fact they are actually quite the opposite. As the psychologist Miller Mair points out, an individual is actually "a community of selves",[32] each of them adapted to a particular interpersonal or transpersonal function, thus allowing that individual to perform properly and yet still be themselves. Personal integrity requires this flexibility of selfhood; without it community could not exist and people would have to abandon their identity as human beings.

A real self, then, is an adaptable one, and we are all in a position to choose which aspect of our multi-faceted personality is appropriate for a particular interpersonal situation. Our motives may be honest or dishonest, but the action of role assumption will be both familiar and natural. The same holds when the role is entirely imaginary, as it is in the theatre; although here imagination has to find ways of giving itself the body of an actual human being, what Stanislavski calls "building a character".[33] The honesty of this enterprise depends entirely on the theatre's willingness to admit the deception involved in passing off an (actual) actor as an (imaginary) character; but as far as the actors are concerned, they are simply adapting their own inalienable selfhood to meet a specification with which they are already familiar.

The hard work in developing a role, then, is associated with tracing the relationship which exists between script and plot; in other words, the lines provided for a character and the circumstances in which she or he is supposed to deliver them, two things which belong together as the actor begins to become increasingly familiar with the world of the play, moving back and forth between two frames of reference. The world of the play takes on substance as a result of the creative interaction between the lines and the reason for them, and their expression in movement and gesture.

Actors say that they memorise their lines by fitting word and movement together, as speech is triggered by emotion and the bodily gestures immediately associated with it. Thus movement and gesture signal feeling, and this gives rise to words. In the same way, the story to be acted out is fictional, but the location provided for its enactment is not; whatever it may represent, in itself it is intensely real, somewhere to move into and stand, sit, lie etc., all of them actions or bodily dispositions able to carry speech along with them. Thus, actors engaged in learning lines will imagine the part of the stage in which they say something and consequently their motive for being there to say it.

This proprioceptive memorising of lines belongs to the inductive process of role-appropriation on which theatre itself depends. It is sometimes assumed that the ability to act and to learn lines are two separate skills, so that in order to be an actor a person needs a good memory and a powerful imagination. Remembering and pretending are certainly essential, but neither is much use without the other, and it is the power to do both at the same time which is the secret of acting, or indeed of anything to do with theatre. Whereas audiences are not required to learn lines they must certainly pay attention to storylines, which they could never do and would see no point in doing without a *mise en scène* supplied by imagination and held in place by memory. Imagination is itself rooted in past experience of events perceived imaginatively.

The exchange of roles between theatre and life is by no means straightforward. Jacques is certainly right to say that people at various stages of their lives resemble actors who have taken on a particular role, that of someone of the age in question, and that each stage in life opens itself to certain stereotypical ways of presenting oneself. Thinking of life's various stages, Jacques is reminded of the theatre. Because he is who he is, someone with a particular personality, he proceeds to share his insight. (Also, of course, because this is a play and the person playing Jacques is an actor.)

In such a way Jacques draws our attention to the multi-layered working of theatrical role play, to which the subject of time-bound human identity provides a particularly memorable introduction. Drama speaks to us in such a way that a vivid image directs us to an entire vista of meanings which are separate yet connected. Using the language of drama, one shining example stands as "cipher to a great accompt".[34] The roles which Jacques distinguishes remind us all of role-playing, every kind of participation in the shared project of theatre, where roles are reversed and exchanged so that relationship emerges. Obviously there is a difference between the roles we are involved in playing in our daily lives and those prescribed for people taking part in an actual play, but there is also an obvious similarity; and it is precisely this ambiguity which captures our imagination, making Jacques's words so memorable: not simply for their sardonic humour and acute observation, but also because this is an actor who is speaking them.

Perhaps this is why we are so willing to use theatrical language in ordinary conversation, and speak of 'upstaging' someone, or 'coming in on cue', or 'ringing down the curtain'. Metaphors like these are intended to make what we want to say more vivid and give it 'colour'. In fact what they do is widen its scope and render it transparent. There are other metaphors we might use, this being the major purpose of metaphor, but we seize on the theatre because of its explicitly figurative role in heightening awareness to see beyond itself. Theatre manages to be both concrete and evocative, vague and yet specific: it is an embodied metaphor that springs immediately to mind whenever we feel the need to stress the significance of things which happen to us.

The ambiguity of theatre, the metaphorical resonance associated with it, resists the impulse to limit it to a demonstration of contrasting social roles or character types. Even those playwrights whose work revolves round these differences and whose plots hinge on them – Ben Jonson, Molière, the writers of Restoration comedy, for example – depend for dramatic effect on their characters' ability to act uncharacteristically on occasion, so that the unforeseen may happen and a carefully constructed world fall apart. Far from reinforcing current social arrangements, these plays exist to draw our attention to the danger of taking such things seriously; the same goes for human personality whose fascination lies in variation rather than regularity.

Because they depend in some or other form of unexpectedness, whether the effect is tragic, comic or merely embarrassing, roles can never be easy to tie down. This is what actors themselves say:

> I always seem to myself to be surprised by what I say or perhaps by the way I say it, which always seems to come from somewhere else in the character I'm playing. I think this is how the character grows, almost without any assistance on my part.

This actor was new to the profession, but I have often heard the same thing from those usually classified as 'old stagers'.

> As time went on I learned more and more to trust the person I'm playing and allow him to go wherever it is he wants to go without me getting too much in the way. If you see what I mean.

One night she seems to be one person, and the next night someone else! I'm not quite sure who she is tonight . . .

This last actor was talking about the role she was playing. She was anxious because the character seemed to have taken on a life of its own. In the course of learning their profession actors are warned of the danger of not being able to leave your part behind you at the stage door. Their job is to move from play to play, so they certainly cannot afford to get too involved with any of the people whom they have to impersonate. Part of the skill of acting, they are reminded, is to preserve the distinction between ordinary life and the world of the play, the alternative being a kind of madness in which you lose all sense of who you yourself are.

There is obviously a good deal of sense in this, yet all the same the fact remains that it is always a counsel of perfection. Actors are bound to be affected by some of the characters with whom they are requested to identify themselves. Just as we learn from one another in life, so we pick up ideas and attitudes of mind from characters in plays – particularly if we ourselves have to pretend to *be* those characters. The character itself, of course, has no independent existence. What comes to life in the play is the role-playing aspect of the person who plays the part, something that is both adaptable and highly inventive. If we imagine that the role is insidiously asserting itself at our own expense, then we should reflect on the fact that this is what roles tend to do. Their function is to carry out a particular task as efficiently as possible, in this case that of giving life to a fictional character such as Jacques himself.

6

PRIVATE SPACE

It left me with a feeling of sadness at the way people treat their parents. I've daughters too, you see, two of them married, and so I feel vulnerable. Growing old leaves you very unprotected . . .

This story left a definite mark on how I think about myself, bringing home how self-centred I have always been. This man saw all the world in terms of himself, so that his three daughters were simply part of his domain . . .

We see the world from our own point of view. The two people above are reporting on the same play, yet seeing it completely differently. In this they were in the same position as the other members of the audience, each of whom was left with her or his own more or less separate and individual version of Shakespeare's *King Lear* which they would be prepared to defend as the play's real meaning. After all, this is the way we have been taught to look at things – as if their significance were something belonging to themselves, and our job is therefore to recognise it and identify its usefulness for any purpose to which it may be put.

However, as Heidegger points out, meaning is not intrinsic to phenomena but bestowed on them in the act of interpretation, which is something that is carried out by human beings: "Two men look through the same bars, One sees the mud, and one the stars".[35] In fact, the action of making sense and that of perceiving are the same, so that everything depends on the view we find ourselves taking, as what we see is determined by how we look. This, however, is decided very

40

largely by a personal tendency to see things in a particular way, according to the associations they have for each individual. "A rose, is a rose, is a rose," said the poet,[36] but roses mean different things to different people.

The cognitive psychologist George Kelly[37] describes this in terms of 'personal construct systems': Thus we judge the relative significance of things which happen to us by identifying the position which they, and things like them, occupy in their own private hierarchy of importance – vital things at the top, less important ones lower down, but all linked together by the system which orders them. Because there are bound to be more relatively unimportant things than the obviously important ones, the whole system may be seen as a kind of pyramid of values, a way in which we can gauge the worth of our experiences; that is, their value to ourselves.

It is important to realise that these 'value clusters' are not permanently fixed. The connections become looser and more flexible as they progress down the system. The top-most value, which Kelly refers to as the 'regnant construct', is not likely to change very much whatever may happen to the person who holds to it, but lower down the scale attitudes which are less entrenched may be modified by events and the learning which they carry with them. Since the way we look at life depends on the entire system which we have put together and not on a single dominant value, we shall find ourselves changing our minds on less important matters. Each time we do this, our personal blueprint for making sense grows more comprehensive, as we grow less exclusive in our way of viewing the world we are living in, and consequently in assessing the significance of the things which happen to us in it, all of which differ according to the circumstances involved and our own interpretation of them.

The two audience-members who had been drawn imaginatively into the same scenario managed to see two completely different plays, both significant for the individual concerned. Even a story as succinct and tightly plotted as *King Lear* allowed this to happen. Each of these dramas was about fatherhood and involved daughters. Both were powerful enough to give rise to a genuinely emotional experience, able to add its weight to ideas and assumptions regarding fathers and daughters which were already alive within the audience, so that it could be said that, from this point of view, several hundred people managed to be present at the same number of plays, each of them in important personal ways different from the others.

This is not so ridiculous as it may seem. Theatre is essentially unspecific, its meaning closer to poetry than to mathematics. No-one tells a story in such circumstances expecting it to be taken literally, for if that were to happen it would cease to be a story and become simply a description, useful for information and little else. Shakespeare intended his play to be understood as fiction, thus leaving it susceptible to the private fictions of others – their ability to understand human behaviour in terms of their own way of making sense of it. The meaning of a play remains in a volatile condition however firmly its author tries to grasp it. This is not to suggest that Shakespeare himself may not have known what he was doing, but that we should not always be certain that we ourselves do.

Viewed from this angle, the play may act as an *agent provocateur*. Certainly no playwright knows what effect his or her play will have when it is performed, or what any particular person in the audience is likely to make of it, although they themselves may well have definite views as to the kind of response they would prefer. It may be the author's or director's intention to guide the audience towards certain conclusions which they feel are suggested by the story; but whether such a thing will happen, and to what extent, no-one can be sure. The kind of reassurance which they are looking for is not available in theatre. In both a literal and metaphorical sense, space is provided; and with it, room for uncertainty.

Starting with the author, this space-making function of theatre includes everyone involved with the play's presentation, the audience participating in a shared world along with the actors. At the same time, theatre not only creates space but uses it, seizing hold of every opportunity to invite us into the space it has made available, handing it over to us to be used in any way we choose, so that we may find one which makes sense to us, rather than anyone else, even the author. This is the freedom which lies at the heart of the theatre, to give us space to explore ourselves in a way which nothing else can.

Certainly, to put it like this seems to overstate the case, for everyone involved in working on a play is eager to remain as close as possible to the author's intention; or if this is considered to be reasonably clear, to make an interesting or provocative comment on it by the way they are presenting it. It would be absurd to suggest that the intended message never gets across; of course, it does, but in many versions, not all of which could be recognised by its presenters. In an abstract way, what the play is about, its main theme, is certainly likely to register. *King Lear*, for instance, is about rejection: its central image, what Brecht calls its *"grund-gestus"*,[38] that is an old man shaking his fist at the heavens. This iconic moment is strong enough in itself to trigger a range of emotions apart from the guilt and vulnerability seized on by the two audience members, as each person witnessing it does so from a completely different point of view, as they find themselves reliving experiences unique to themselves.

Nevertheless, Lear's gesture would be without meaning for us if we were so imprisoned by individuality that we could not respond to communality, or so taken up with difference that we failed to respond to similarity. We may not be able to reproduce the exact emotion required by the playwright, conditioned as this is by a specific set of circumstances which is unique to the play, but we can certainly produce our own version of it, even if this originates within a more private situation. Feeling responds to feeling, as recollection becomes empathy and imagination builds a temporary home for them both. We feel for and with King Lear, and our emotional involvement makes us take what he says and does very seriously. The conclusions we draw will be our own, because this is the author's intention: his plays are stories not instruction manuals. Fables they may certainly be, and sometimes parables, but whatever comes across to us is our own concern. The stories are made out of people rather than propositions, which is why, like members of the audience, they give differing accounts of themselves rather than offering an agreed statement.

This freedom to react and interpret is another aspect of theatre's space-creating function. Theatre makes room for responses which are authentically personal because they have been matured in individual and group memory. This does not mean they are unchangeable, for memories are continually readjusted to take account of fresh experience, just as our ways of judging values are modified, if not changed by events. Theatre uses its freedom in order to affect the way we see ourselves even if it does not set out consciously to transform it. By doing this it increases the freedom we ourselves enjoy, the space needed for living.

If we see ourselves as having not only one self but several, we will need room to spread ourselves in order to make the best of who we

43

are. This is the psychological process which Jung describes as "integration" of selfhood.[39] Because we concentrate too much on developing a single aspect of our personality, the one which we have come to regard as appropriate or even necessary for the role we are playing in life, we neglect the potential we all possess for diversification of the selves we can imagine being, if we could give ourselves permission to do so. As Jung says, this is not easy; all the same, it is certainly possible. Moreover, for real psychological growth it is actually necessary for us to expend some effort trying to achieve it.

Jung is mainly concerned here with unconscious truths, but even at the cognitive level our aptitude for imitating other people's states of mind and at least experimenting with aspects of their personalities gives plausibility to the idea that we are at least potentially capable of being more than one kind of person ourselves, although we have been trained to reject the possibility as incompatible with a view of mental health which defines it as an ability to be quite sure who you think you ought to be. What is involved here, however, is not confusion of identity but the refusal to accept evidence regarding multiplicity. What can scarcely be disputed is that a sense of opportunity to increase awareness accompanies the way human beings learn about themselves and other people. Once this has been taken up, the result is our own version of whatever we have learned; in other words we include it in the space our selfhood occupies, which expands to make room for it and diversifies in accordance with the nature of what it takes in.

In this sense we are certainly representative of a huge number of influences, some of which have developed more personally than others, even to the point of our bestowing on them a quasi-independent identity: "That's my father in me, I suppose," we say. To identify with someone in this personal way is to enlist them as companion selves, so adding to the invisible community which we are conscious of representing. This is the group of selves which, Miller Mair says, need to be understood and taken seriously so that they may continue to keep us psychologically alive.[40] They themselves belong to our unique selfhood, helping us make sense of our journey; the space they inhabit is the interior landscape through which they and we are moving.

Of all the arts, theatre embodies this the most vividly. Theatre shows us space which expands and contracts with those who inhabit it, and is brought to life and laid to rest in tune with events taking place and feelings expressed there. In theatre these two spaces, the self and the stage, encounter each other, coming together because they have room to do so, each having given the other permission. Both spaces are, of course, imaginary ones, as this is the means we naturally use to create the space which we need in order to look at ourselves properly; we stand back in order to see more clearly. In the same way we also look at other people, using imagination as a space shared by ourselves and them, one which both separates and unites; a place of meeting, set aside for personal encounter, giving rise by its nature to the possibility of intimacy, both with ourselves and others.

By its nature it is imagination which does the work for us. All we have to do is allow it to exert the strength which it possesses. In plays we give it permission to act for us, agreeing to take it more seriously than we are usually in the habit of doing, admitting to ourselves, in fact, that our imagination is important to us, and showing willingness to confess this to other people by publicly displaying the consequences of its presence. Whether conscious or not, the freedom to respond in different ways is of immense importance to theatre. This is not to say that, in itself, emotion is not contagious, but that it refers to things which are regarded by each individual as unique to themselves and which only they possess – an inalienable characteristic of the person whom they know themselves to be.

For each of these, the play must be allowed to be a personal event, something directly addressed to them; or rather, it must be interpretable by them as such. This is the only way that they can get anything from it. Sometimes they are aware during the play itself of some personal relevance which it holds for them; frequently this happens at the end when the lights have gone up and they reflect on whether or not they consider the experience to have been worthwhile, perhaps comparing it with other plays which they remember: "It really managed to get through to me." Such things definitely seem to stay in the mind. They are the reason why, having once come, we are eager to repeat the experiment.

In fact they are the reason for our co-operation in the enterprise of theatre itself, our eagerness to 'suspend our disbelief'. This is more than the simple willingness to give permission for something to happen to us without offering any kind of resistance. It is a definite intention to imagine in a way which will agree with whatever the play is about to offer; to make room for it by bracketing our own interior dramas so that these will not intervene to the exclusion of the one in which our presence is required. These private theatres of our own are to be temporarily closed rather than permanently demolished, and the play-space we have chosen to enter is one which may well turn out to provide its own version of some very familiar scenery. Even so, when the time comes to leave it we do so.

We manage not to leave empty handed, however. There is always something to discuss, both with ourselves and other people. This, too, is part of the enjoyment of theatre – the movement between spaces, private into public and back again into private, as the play we have shared itself becomes material for our own personal playmaking, to be taken seriously or not according to how it fits the story which we discern emerging from our own lives. One way or another, the play we have been involved with for a short time is bound to have its effect on us; but what that effect will be we have no possible way of telling in advance.

This kind of personal freedom, to decide what is important to oneself and why it should be so important, is not only a principal subject for plays of all kinds; it is the message communicated by the theatre itself. This is a space left free on purpose. Just as the author used it for what he or she desired to give, so may we for what we would like to receive. However clear the author's meaning may be, we are under no obligation to interpret it along what other people consider to be the right lines. Whether we do or not, the encounter will be a liberating one, for theatre is a holism of overlapping interpretations held together by a single, original, creative vision. It is no kind of lecture or demonstration but a communion of selves.

7

FUNCTIONAL SPACE

I've seen this play twice and actually been in it twice as well, and when Caesar gets stabbed I still think maybe this time it's not going to happen. I look at the conspirators and think perhaps they won't manage to pull it off this time.

The purpose of theatre is to make space for exploring human relationship in an imaginative way. Using imagination like this affords it a public dignity in addition to its familiar function as a way of testing hypotheses, a safe substitute for actual behaviour. In theatre we allow it to make an appearance centre-stage instead of keeping it hidden behind scenes for our own private use. We have of course to give it something to wear. We are already familiar with stories because of the ones we are used to telling to ourselves and sometimes others as well, of course. Now, however, we undertake to involve a wider audience in the corporate gesture by which imagination is shared.

Earlier, we were looking at the way in which incidents in plays give rise to feelings which are powerful enough to fix them in our memories even when the original story has been largely forgotten. Not all stories fade easily, however; and this is why they are stories and not merely accounts of events recorded in chronological order. To tell a story, mere narration is not enough. For one thing, narratives only stop when conditions force them to do so, just as war correspondents finish their reports at the TV news presenter's signal. Stories, on the other hand, stop when their ending has been reached. Stories have endings; it is the most important thing about them. Like sentences, they make complete statements, saying what they want to say and marking it off from anything else which might be said. What the story has to tell us depends on the events it recounts hanging together in the space set aside for them, that is the one delineated by and contained by a beginning and an ending.

A conclusion, in fact. We do not know what to think, how to react, until the story finishes and the full stop has been reached. Like a word or phrase within a sentence, an action or episode in a play is incapable of telling us the full story. We said as much when we were looking at the shape of theatre. If we want to draw *our* conclusions then we must wait for the actual one; that is, the one given by *the play itself*, which may not be all we want to say but is certainly all that the play intends showing us.

All it wants to show us now, that is. The play as it stands is all that the author and his collaborators engaged in the arduous yet fascinating task of presenting it to us actually want us to see. Take this, they say; it is all we have to offer, but you are welcome to take it home if you wish to do so. If we were to ask them about the story told by the play, why this or that was not shown although it had been mentioned; saying that we had been left wondering what was going to happen to the characters now the lights had gone out on an empty stage, we are quite likely to be told that such things are not actually their business. They would be wrong, however, because leaving this kind of information out is precisely their business, which is to provide us with something which we will in fact be in a position to 'take home' because it now has a definite shape, one which we ourselves can handle.

The play as performed, the performance which takes us into itself, is an immediate experience, there for us to immerse ourselves in, if we are willing to allow this to happen. If we are, then we are certainly in a position to do so. What we are experiencing has been designed to engage us in the most personal way by avoiding distractions from the story it presents along with anything else considered capable of reducing its dramatic impact on an audience. Neither we nor the actors are consciously aware of the play's structure during the performance, although an intuitive sense of an underlying shape is certainly present and may sometimes rise to the surface, if only because we know that, having chosen to suspend our disbelief, we ourselves are engaging in a meaningful action, one which itself symbolises meaning: in other words, one which possesses a beginning, a middle and an end.

This is the gift we take away with us, the focused memory of a meaning capable of giving birth to an entire range of alternative interpretations inspired by the revelatory experience of a symbolism which draws its life from the timeless reality to which it points, the truth which lives between persons. We have seen how plays mean different things to different people; without the symbolic integrity all plays possess, which is their individual ability to stand by themselves independently of our interpreting them to suit our own inclinations, we could not use them in the creative way which they are encouraging us to do. As it is, however, plays proclaim their nature in as straightforward a way as possible, revealing their identity as functional artefacts by the way they are constructed and presented. Their job is to involve us in things which we know to be fictional, events in which we ourselves will participate, arranged in order to make a point about human living and dying. The point to be made is one decided by the way the events have been arranged, which is principally the author's own responsibility. It comes across in an authoritative way because the medium itself is designed for this to happen – not to commit itself to a particular message or viewpoint, but to ensure that whatever emerges does so as effectively as possible. As the Bellman assures us, "What I tell you three times is true"[41] – the Bellman in this case being the author.

Although it is inspired by imagination, theatre's truth is underlined by the logic of its structure. Euclid distinguished 3 as "the number of perfection". Because of their characteristic configuration, stories assert the cognitive primacy of three-ness,[42] according to which things which have a beginning, a middle and an end are known to possess the significance ascribed to completeness: they are recognised as whole in themselves and so may be taken into account when we consider other things. We may not like them or approve of their existence, but there is no doubt that, for us, they certainly figure. For this reason, three-ness is paradigmatic of messages received and understood, whether or not we ourselves choose to take them as personally applicable: all function according to what could be described as 'the principle of triplicity'.

If this is the case with stories, it is certainly also true of the plots of plays. They possess a self-ascribed truthfulness inherent in the way in which they have been put together. Consequently they act as witnesses to themselves in a way which is able to undermine argument, or at least seriously shake our trust in it. From this point of view, our own opinion of what a play is about bows to what the plot shows it to be saying, so that the conclusion we reach always reflects our awareness of this, even to the extent of being an alternative version of the authorised one. Our own interpretation certainly stays with us – it is after all our own; but running parallel with it is the play's own three-fold message about itself: "What I tell you three times is true." After all, our versions reflect what we ourselves prefer; and are always to this extent a compromise which, under the circumstances, represents all we can manage.

The audience member quoted at the beginning of the chapter still clung with part of himself to an alternative *Julius Caesar* – or at least the possibility for one – in which the shocking event being re-enacted would simply not happen. At the same time he was fully cognisant of the fact that this would not actually take place; not only because the play he was immersed in was demonstrably the same one which he had seen (and acted in) previously, but also owing to the unshakeable logic of its plot, which in spite of his private dreaming, remained powerful enough to carry him along with it. "It wasn't that I couldn't bear Caesar to be assassinated," he told me, "but that I always seem to have somehow forgotten that it is actually going to happen." The truth was, of course, that in the world governed by the plot the occasion for this had not yet arrived, and those who were taking part either as actors or audience were, on this and every other performance of *Julius Caesar*, mainly concerned to go along with the story.

In fact, the assertiveness of the story plays an important role in making room for itself within the flow of our experience. In order to make itself heard, it clears a space in our imagination wide enough for its own story of events and any versions which we might find ourselves devising. In this the plot itself makes room for us, as it sets our imaginations at work in the way it works itself, encouraging the creativity from which it originally arose. This is the space which empowers; space as opportunity, the chance for new things to come into existence. The story embodied in the play is itself an enabling milieu, nurturing its own imaginative life, both in the play itself and within the hearts and minds of those involved, whether on-stage or in the audience. Thus the space of theatre is not just perceived – either literally or in symbolic form – but is also expressed in the way we actually think. The play gives us space for our own thought. Even when we find ourselves at odds with what the play clearly means us to be thinking, the authority with which drama is able to present its case draws us into the argument in order to put the other side of the story. What is being acted out is convincing on its own terms and so we are willing for the time being to collude, leaving our intellect 'waiting in the wings'. The wings too, of course are a vitally important part of theatre.

Books such as this are written in the space created by the plots of plays. We write about what we remember and, more to the point, what we look forward to experiencing again. Periods of disengagement reach out for remembered contact, striving somehow to recapture the timeless moment of engagement when the world somehow came to life. We can say, more or less, how it happened; that is, we can describe what it actually *was*, for this takes us into the world of 'as if' – so that we find ourselves apologising for using poetry rather than prose, which is the recognised language of facts. Sometimes, however, we are brought face to face with the fact that there are aspects of human experience, times in our lives which, without poetry, would risk being lost for ever.

Martin Buber in *I and Thou* puts the case for this in a way which is unforgettable:

> The Chinese poet tells how men did not wish to hear the tune he played on his jade flute; then he played it to the gods and they inclined their ears; since then men also listened to the tune: thus he went from the gods to those whom the 'structure' cannot dispense with.[43]

The poet's melody and the flute belonged together. They were part of the structure in the sense that one of them was no use without the other (and jade is a very hard material). All the same, neither was able to function as it ought without assistance from outside – that is, from a source of life and inspiration which by definition remains other than literal. Writing about theatre is a lifeless occupation without the occasional presence of things which no longer have any current existence. If we were to try to live within these presences all the time, nothing would actually get written down; but refusing to acknowledge them leaves nothing really worth writing about. These moments which stand out so vividly for us were the ones when, leaving self-consciousness behind, we made contact with a life which was not our own and we were caught up in it, living it as ours. These are theatre's 'Thou' moments and we treasure them.

"Rarely, rarely, comest thou / Spirit of delight".[44] We touch but cannot grasp; for whenever we set our minds to it we manage to change its nature into 'It'. This is the sphere of things we do and carry on doing. In terms of theatre these are the technicians' skill and the artists' talent, the theatre building and the presence of the audience. When the play comes alive for us it does so in relation to these things rather than as something created by them. We certainly need them, just as the poet needs his jade flute: if they are not the life of the play, they are the air which it breathes. The play's life is that which moves in the space they provide; the breathing space. The structure gives it room to move freely, so that it can come and go without restriction. Buber reminds us that "the attitude of man is two-fold":[45] as contact inevitably gives rise to experience, so the opposite also happens and we are carried forward by the things we make into encounters previously unimagined. Just as 'It' depends on 'Thou' for its life, 'Thou' depends on 'It' to provide the opportunities it needs. Art, Buber points out, is the most striking evidence of this, providing space for 'It' to give birth to 'Thou'.

In theatre, the action of the plot does not only unfold, it enfolds. Once we have placed ourselves in its hands, the story takes over. By leading, it also grounds us. As an infant trusts the floor on which it crawls, so we, having made our own initial commitment to an imaginary world, are determined to go wherever the story has already mapped out for us. Having promised not to doubt, we cling to our promise, so that even if we have been along this particular road on previous occasions and actually know it quite well, we are unwilling to admit the fact because travelling in this way is always fascinating, even if not necessarily enjoyable. Our enjoyment changes, however, with the movements of the plot, which has been specifically designed so that we shall always be surprised by what may turn out to be around the corner. In the meantime we go on obediently suspending our disbelief.

The plot itself needs room to manoeuvre and will give itself the space required to do so. Its inventiveness is only partly its own, inspired as it was by the encounter in which it itself originated, as 'It' became 'Thou' in the imagination of the author. In theatre the exchange of focus which characterises our awareness as individual human beings is more recognisable than elsewhere because by writing and performing plays we have set out to make it so, demonstrating to ourselves an oscillation between acceptance and estrangement, alienation and belonging – advance and retreat – which is so natural to us that we scarcely notice it happening. It is not something we think about, if only because thought itself is only one side of the equation and tends to turn us in towards ourselves, away from the otherness which alone makes it creative. Theatre was devised to give life to thought, by encouraging us to draw attention to what might otherwise be overlooked: the living connection between people themselves and our ideas about them.

In order to do this space is central, both as idea and actuality. Theatre both makes use of space and actually creates it; or rather, it makes use of it by the action of creating it, for theatre is itself a space cleared in life to allow us to concentrate our attention on the business of living, an activity occluded from our sight by the many things which preoccupy us, the chief of which is the fears aroused by our own vulnerability. Just as fear distances us from life, theatre distances us from fear. By so doing it gives us a breathing space to recoup our power to reach out in fellowship to others of our own kind – to reach across.

How we make use of this space is, of course, entirely up to us. The only demand the space makes is that we should recognise it as itself; that is, as something which offers us the freedom needed to appreciate its emptiness and take account of the opportunity it gives for us to find some way or other of filling it. Because it is at present empty, we naturally find it both alarming and inviting, for just as the presence of others may inhibit us, so also does their absence. We are conscious of a need to express ourselves by taking up the opportunity it appears to be holding out to us. This is why, if the space is clearly designed for a story, and the one occupying it is already well known, we may find ourselves turning down its invitation to take part, preferring one of our own: hence the temptation to flirt with alternative outcomes mentioned earlier. This is not something to be interpreted as disloyalty to the author's intention, a betrayal of the plot. It is precisely the plot's toughness which allows us to make the story our own.

8

SPACE TO MANOEUVRE

If I've got to choose, I go for comedy rather than tragedy. I'd rather be made to laugh than cry; and the same goes for films and TV. (Overheard in a theatre queue.)

Although this book has not attempted to deal with medical aspects of theatre, throughout its course the healing of persons has been a recurrent theme. Looking at the way theatre gives people the opportunity to rediscover themselves we have continually had to pay attention to the need for it to make space for such a thing to happen. If the objection were made, as it might well be, that space is used for any number of purposes apart from the presentation of plays, so there is no need to single out theatrical space as a medium for healing, the reply must be that the connection here is justified by the fact that it is the absence or denial of a particular kind of space that necessary for us to relate to one another as human beings, which affects our psychological health in ways which are frequently either misunderstood or simply ignored.

Perhaps there are many reasons for this neglect. One of them, however, concerns our way of looking at things nowadays, reinforced by the presence of huge commercial edifices we have erected to support a particular attitude of mind. This is the assumption that work and enjoyment are somehow opposed to each other, so that pleasure must always be effortless or at least as effortless as we can make it. The idea that the aim of human labour must be to get rid of the need for its own existence has always had a powerful effect on the way in which we feel, think and behave, as a chimera devoted to the elimination of whatever it is we believe to be the cause of our malaise.

Why we are never completely satisfied with the outcome is because we have been working in the wrong direction. We have mis-diagnosed ourselves: it is not work which is our sickness but our conviction that everything should somehow be made easy, because human happiness depends on not having to make too much effort to achieve it.

Somehow we go on clinging to this delusion against the evidence. We know that satisfaction derives from achievement but prefer to go on pretending that life would be improved for us if we managed to demonstrate that, on this occasion and in our case, the fact does not apply. Our sickness is not laziness but cowardice – fear of being put to the test, challenged in some way which might turn out to be beyond our powers. We comfort ourselves with half-hearted assurances that by avoiding having to face whatever it is which confronts us, not letting it be a 'problem' to us, we will somehow manage to stay out of trouble. Indeed this is one reason why we go to the theatre; because by doing so we can satisfy ourselves that it is actually possible to keep life at a distance.

It must be admitted that such an attitude appears to be reasonable. Theatre certainly shows us varying degrees of human difficulty, from embarrassment to total defeat. Moreover, it presents these things happening to people for whom we would not be personally responsible *even if they were real*. Above all one thing stands out as being certainly the case: even if some may turn out to look and sound familiar, they are not in fact ourselves. We are perfectly entitled to relax, sit back and enjoy the difference. Isn't this, after all, what theatres were erected for in the first place?

Certainly theatres are concerned with difference, but their aim is not to increase its effects but overcome them. To do this difference is used against itself, an aesthetic distancing countering one which is psychological so that estrangement becomes encounter. Theatrical distancing is the space in which this reconciliation is allowed to take effect, the safe space of shared imagining. What we so often see as an escape from involvement is a way of embracing it. Its effectiveness is not dependent on our original state of mind or our reason for going in the first place; the difference between theatre and our own private perception of reality opens a space in our awareness for attitudes and feelings which ordinarily go unquestioned. Under these special circumstances, we begin to react to life differently. The occasion involves fiction, but the reaction is certainly real and actual. This it is we remember and take back home with us.

We remember the experience because, in fact, we worked so hard to get it. Sharing someone else's burden can be arduous; it 'takes it out of us' we say, thereby acknowledging our own existing needs for relief from the emotional burdens we bear. Apart from this and prior to it, is the effect to be made to overcome a natural disinclination to allow ourselves to get involved, either with others' pain or, by reflection, our own. We expect that, knowing all the time that what is going on here cannot legitimately be considered as 'for real', we should therefore really find it quite easy – which, after all, is our reason for allowing it to happen to us.

In fact, of course, is does 'ease' us, but at a price, one we find ourselves called on to pay in terms of our consenting to be led, in imagination, into places we usually prefer not to visit. Perhaps we assume that the imaginary nature of the circumstances will be an adequate protection against taking these things seriously. If so, we are only deceiving ourselves. Imagination follows its own rules: if we enter willingly we open ourselves to sharing other people's pain, but if we hold back and refuse to join in, we feel somehow deprived or even frustrated, as if we have been cheated of the satisfaction we were expecting. Either way there is discomfort; we must move out of a position which is neither tenable nor tolerable. We have put ourselves in a place where we have no intention of staying and we know that, one way or another we must move out of it.

In fact it is impossible for us not to move from here, and there are only two directions in which to go. The first one is to cut our losses and walk away, actually leaving the theatre building. The second is to move further into what is happening in the play. The first is physical, the second imagined; both are actions which reveal a conscious intention on our part to leave the position which we were formerly in and go somewhere else. Theatres exist because the second is so much easier to do than the first, as anyone who has walked out during a performance is aware. To allow ourselves to be drawn into the action is not hard, however, if that is what we have decided to do; after all, isn't that what we came to the theatre for?

The first reaction described above, that of getting up and walking out of the theatre, is comparatively uncommon. In itself it is a kind of performance and a particularly dramatic one as well, having all the emotional power which we are used to associating with the theatre. As such it is regarded as a last resort, both by the person themselves and by the other members of the audience whose attention has been seized by this vivid example of theatre making its own space. The same principle, however, is at work to counter any impulse we may have to dishonour the agreement we have made to collaborate with the play to the best of our ability by at least remaining in our seats, as the space created by our imaginative involvement in the emergent play-world holds us in too firm a grip. It is the space which holds us, even before we have had time to lose ourselves in anything which may happen there. As we have already seen, the first action of any drama is to make space for itself. It cannot do so by itself, however, which is why it depends on our willingness to accept the invitation to make ourselves present. This collusive action on our part is theatre's initial space-making gesture, from which everything else flows.

These are all things which we, the people who go to see plays, know already, of course. You might even say that we are familiar with them, so that we take them for granted as part of the overall experience of 'going to the theatre'. It is by no means hard to do this because the occasion seems to us to be self-contained, something which starts at the box office and finishes some time later on the pavement outside the theatre, and consists in itself of a completed action, a story with a beginning and an end. (The same is true, of course, when we switch on the television set at the exact time to 'catch' the play for which we have been waiting.)

What we do remember, however, is whether or not we enjoyed the experience, either at the time or afterwards. Quite possibly we were uncomfortable during parts of the play but valued the experience in retrospect. This latter reaction is a common one, as it appears that a major part of the satisfaction we draw from theatre lies in our sense of having worked through the play alongside the characters in it. The various painful situations which they encountered are the times we enjoyed least, which is not surprising considering our commitment to sharing their experiences with them. We may tell ourselves that this is only happening in our imagination; but where else does anyone ever feel emotional pain?

If we think of ourselves as motivated solely by a search for pleasure and have come to the theatre hoping for unalloyed entertainment, we will be challenged by the suggestion that we should be willing to share painful or difficult emotions 'for the play's sake', an expectation which underlies every kind of theatre from grand opera to *commedia dell'arte* – everywhere that there is a story worth sharing because of its relevance to the emotional life of all taking part. Theatre helps us rise to the challenge presented to us by feelings which we do not want reminding about by carrying us on its way into calmer water. Looking back on the experience we are grateful for it, but not really very sure we want to repeat it. Next time, we say to ourselves, we will settle for something a little easier, perhaps.

Locations created and kept separate are associated with situations which are personally challenging. In fact they are dedicated to them: university examination rooms and doctors' surgeries are a case in point. So, of course, are shrines and other explicitly religious locations. These are places whose purpose necessarily involves the idea of important changes taking place in people's lives. They symbolise the necessity for movement, and their claim upon the imagination is powerful enough to implant the idea of personal change as an active presence in our awareness. The initiatory purpose which lies at the heart of religious ritual suggests that all these separated places are to be understood as at least implicitly religious.[46] No wonder, then, that theatre is able to disturb our composure in the way which it does, being the most intensely focused of all dedicated spaces.

Theatre, then, is capable of making demands on us which we feel obliged to resist, mainly those associated with our need to change in some way or other. We do not have to take any notice of them, of course; but if we ignore them completely, there is always the suspicion, or even in some cases the suggestion that if this is the case we are engaged in wasting our time. The woman in the theatre queue went on to say that, if she chose the comedy rather than the play which threatened to be more serious she always felt slightly disappointed "as though I made the wrong decision". There is a very definite conviction, nurtured by drama presentations on television, that plays are not simply entertainment, but really, as she put it, "about life".

We do not go to the theatre in order to be changed. At a conscious level the question does not usually arise, even if we admit to some awareness of the need for a degree of change in the way we view ourselves and the world about us. Unlike religion, theatre does not require us to place ourselves entirely in its hands, giving it full permission to mould us in any way it chooses. What it does do, however, is introduce us to change as an available human experience rather than an abstract idea by including us in a life-change happening here and now, right among us; not permanently involving us, but allowing us to feel, *from the inside*, those existential challenges which we sometimes try so hard to avoid. Often the anxiety we feel at the prospect of an evening of 'serious' theatre refers to plays which we have not yet seen, and so involves the idea of theatre rather than its actuality. Those who can look back on having survived the play and have since felt reassured by the experience will be less alarmed by the expectation of reliving it; although this largely depends, of course, on the measure of their original involvement; those who admit that for them the play really 'worked' will look forward to the opportunity of seeing it again.

On the face of it this may seem surprising. If an experience is unpleasant and gives rise to anxiety, we would expect a certain unwillingness to have to put up with it again. The reason why so many people choose to do exactly that is because what they remember is not the anxiety – which they are used to feeling – but the release from it, which may be less familiar to them. They associate serious theatre with reduced anxiety, a condition of the mind which is often unaffected by simply being invited to 'have a good laugh'.

As we have seen, theatre brings us face to face with fears which have remained unacknowledged and have consequently not been dealt with: how could they have been? It encourages us to share the feelings of those in the play. We must do this whether we ourselves approve of those feelings or not, because unless we try to do this we have little hope of understanding their behaviour, which we need to be able to do in order to make sense of the play. However we are unable to do it unless we ourselves try to imagine what they are experiencing, something which is not as easy to manage as we may think it ought to be – after all, we are used to trying to work out what our fellow human beings think, feel and intend. Why should it be any different with regard to the personages within the drama? After all, they are supposed to be the same species as ourselves and we should have no difficulty relating to them as we do to anyone else.

In fact things rarely turn out like this. In the protected atmosphere of the theatre our awareness of the dynamics of personal relationship is intensified: we are more than usually conscious of our own individuality and the otherness of anyone not ourselves. It is this differentiation of selves which we find ourselves relinquishing once the play takes hold. Before this can happen, however, an intensified sense of our own individual identity may very well bring into focus some things about us which we prefer to keep well out of sight; and not only that of other people because, far from being a way of avoiding reality, theatre makes it all the more difficult for us to hide from it.

Perhaps this is the most important point to be made regarding the psychological importance of theatre – its ability to transform ideas into happenings. Plays bring us into immediate contact with the subject of our own individual frailty not as an idea to be conveniently forgotten about or even simply ignored, but as a presence to be taken into full account by us: as, in fact, *ourselves*.

This experience, by which theatre helps us engage with our true selves, registers as part of our personal reality because it is self-authenticating; that is, truthful rather than illusory. This is not in any way a sickness in the medical sense of the word, but a characteristic of beings who prefer happiness to sadness, and who, when they are in pain or discomfort look for ways of relieving it. The novelist Barbara Pym[47] speaks of "the vulnerable side that all human beings have". This is the aspect of our personal experience which, through an ability to relieve existential anxiety by conducting us into areas we otherwise avoid, theatre addresses. It does this by simply allowing us to survive, so that we are able to go away reassured.

Contrary to popular opinion, however, this is not something applying only to what people regard as 'serious' theatre. In its own way comedy can be – and often is – just as emotionally challenging as tragedy; it is only that we don't expect it to be. Intentions which are misunderstood, identities which are mistaken, pretensions revealed as absurd or even grotesque, like blown disguises and hiding places which, disastrously, turn out useless, cause audiences as much embarrassment as they do the people within the play – more, in fact, because this embarrassment is not performed but real.[48] This again is the result of vulnerability, of not having as thick a skin as we may have thought we had; it is also the result of the ease with which we imagine ourselves into situations and identities when we know them to be fictional. Plays, whether we classify them as 'heavy' or 'light', somehow manage to 'get under our skin', and to do so more efficiently, more *passionately*, than we give them credit for doing.

It is because they engage with us at this subliminal level that we can be so deeply impressed by their effect on us which is one of reassurance at finding ourselves both understood and accepted.

9

SPACE AS DEPTH

Up to now I have been concentrating on the specific role of space in theatre trying to show how an understanding of this is vital for any attempt we might make to answer the question, "How does theatre work?". We have seen how theatrical space is both opportunity and also gift, an artefact created for the play and also a manifestation of spirit for which the play itself is responsible; something made both *by* and *for* theatre. Thus the impact of theatre has less to do with what it says than how it says it. A serious piece of theatre is one which is seriously theatrical. In other words it is a way of presenting life which takes full advantage of what theatre has to offer.

Clearing a space for something to happen, we perform a symbolic gesture. The action itself is either real or imaginary, its symbolism the power it holds within itself to point to something not yet manifest but already committed to revealing its presence, whether it be a tree, a chair or a human being. Whether we do it in our own minds or within an actual building we make room for theatre stretching the dramatic symbol in order to accommodate our own imaginary world. In this way we clear a space for theatre so that theatre can clear one for us. The acting area itself may be two-dimensional, but its symbolic identity possesses not only extension but depth; hence its fascination for us as a place of disclosure and our consequent willingness to follow where it leads.

The dimension of depth, which acts upon us as the evidence of hiddenness, things as yet unrevealed, suggests profundity. Space becomes a tool for uncovering truths which have been overlooked, crowded out by practicalities. As we have seen, space is opportunity, not only for actual physical movement but for inner progress as well.

Theatre typifies this: on-stage movement, leading the story forward, conducts us deeper into our imaginative world, opening up areas of awareness with which we have remained out of touch, or ones which we have never explored but simply rationalised out of existence.

'Plays bring things back to you.' What is so often said is true not only of things whose existence we have previously recognised, but also ones of which we have never until now taken very much notice. The play, however, makes you aware of them. It points out to you that, in fact, you are yourself familiar with feelings which you have never associated with yourself; which in fact you continue to dissociate yourself from. Once you have made the imaginative leap which theatre asks you to make, you have no option but to face these ancient adversaries. You can no longer continue to write them out of your personal script: someone else has written them in for you. You find yourself under the same scrutiny as the people in the play, while discovering too late that although their world is imaginary, the feelings it evokes are not.

Theatre revives these uncomfortable feelings in us more effectively than anything else is capable of doing. In any play concerned with the experience of being human such feelings must to a large extent dominate not only various episodes but the entire storyline. They are, in fact, the whole point of the play, which concerns the way people react to how they feel about events, for theatre brings all its skills to bear in order to explore a single area of life, that of the impact of affect on behaviour – how the way we feel influences the way we act. What makes theatre so fascinating is the way it directs our attention to connections between action and emotion, or attitude and experience, which are not immediately obvious and which in real-life situations we might very well not notice.

These are the areas of life on which theatre focuses. To do this requires a high degree of concentration. Anything considered likely to prove a distraction from the immediacy of whatever it is that is being looked at must somehow be kept out of the picture. Theatre manages to isolate the rest of life in order to direct attention to a succession of actions which are taking place in our presence and yet outside the limitations imposed by our own time and place. When theatre suggests that we 'work' on our 'imaginary forces' to gain entrance to the scenario presented to us, our first task must be to join with it in excluding everything from our awareness which will make the suspension of disbelief more difficult, isolating the play and ourselves with it from anything likely to detract from its integrity as an alternative reality, at least so far as time, place and personal identity are concerned.

Without this agreement to place imaginary brackets round the rest of the world, theatre could not exist. Of course, neither could any kind of story-telling. It is important to realise, however, that this kind of world-exclusion is never total. Ordinary reality is filtered out rather than completely excluded. Thoughts and feelings remain; it is only situations and the circumstances governing them which are 'put on hold' until the play is over. At the risk of repeating what was said earlier, this fact is of paramount importance, as plays depend on the emotional authenticity of the audience's response and it is the truthfulness of the feelings aroused in us which permits us to make them real, both for ourselves and one another.

The recognisable quality of the feelings and thoughts, attitudes and reactions of the play's characters assures us of the significance of what is happening not only for them but for ourselves as well. This is what grounds the play for us, underlining its intrinsic worth as an important part of our experience of being alive. Thus its emotional resonance acts as convincing evidence of the strength of its claim for our attention. In theatre this is communicated to us by the story-shape of the plot and the imaginative skill of those involved in the play's presentation, whose aim is to remain as faithful as possible to what they regard as its message about what it is to be human.

There is, however, another way in which our belief in the world of the play is strengthened. This too concerns the play's presentation – at the most fundamental of all levels, that of the space made available. The action of focusing on what is happening in our presence within a specific part of the horizon available to our senses requires a definite effort on the part of those presenting the play to preserve the unique nature of that particular location as both open and protected, separate yet contiguous. If the surrounding area is in darkness, that particular part will be illuminated, so that even though it is still part of the surrounding space it will register itself as entirely detached from it. The same applies, of course, for dark places where everything else is brightly lit; but the focusing effect of light is more intense than that of darkness. The contrast symbolises the union of opposites which is theatre itself, where past is joined with present, fact with fiction, metaphor with literal description, matter with spirit.

The focused image opens our way into drama and to everything which exists for us on the far side of the literal. This is the crystallisation of diffuse perceptions which we recognise not only as art, but also spirituality; for theatre can lead us into that dimension of imagination which is the unseen world of the spirit. This, in fact, is its leading role in the drama of human existence, that of 'psychopomp' or 'conductor of souls'. As such it is not the space we look *at*, but the one which we look *through*. This is a property of theatre itself, not only of plays which are explicitly religious or which deal with spirituality as their main subject. The spirituality of theatre is characteristically implicit, waiting to be read into what is happening as well as extracted from it, consisting of the dialogue we ourselves have with the play, one whose outcome must always remain uncertain.

The freedom which lives at the heart of theatre requires that, whatever it may be that arises from this encounter is always 'in the hands of the gods'. Certainly no-one else can ordain what the outcome will be. Audiences have a tendency to resist drawing obvious conclusions, or even ones which the author may be presumed to have intended them to arrive at. The guidance which theatre holds out to us is very basic: we are to pay attention to what goes on in this particular space and to draw our own conclusions. Suggestions of coercion are to be avoided and room left between and among those present: room for spirit. This is to be regarded as the root principle of theatre itself rather than merely a characteristic of particular types of theatre, as for instance Strindberg's *Dream Play*[49] or Classical Greek tragedy. Television soap operas work in the same way; apart from the spirit of free responsiveness, they fail to work at all.

The play's focused action sets us free from distractions in order to contemplate profundity. We do not have to immerse ourselves in whatever lies below the surface, simply to acknowledge its presence. Indeed, it resists the urge to achieve mastery of all we are capable of perceiving, to "seize and clutch and penetrate",[50] as its intention is to direct us towards the unknowable, the mystery surrounding the world as we experience it. Theatre presents us with stories about insoluble problems which in some unexpected way cease to exist, to the amazement of all concerned. This is not because they have been worked out but because they have simply been lived through. In the meantime, however, the world has moved onwards, changing as it goes.

This is a fact about life which never ceases to be mysterious. Theatre is a leading witness to its truthfulness. Without mystery of some kind it is unable to function at all. Its whole existence is testimony to the unpredictable nature of human existence and the situations which arise from this, particularly those involving the future of our efforts to make it predictable. This is the subject matter of theatre, its content; its form is what the play gives to it, or rather what we ourselves bestow on it in the extended process of transforming an idea into a work of art. The outline of such a work strives for some kind of clarity, or at least immediacy. Metaphorically speaking, it says what it intends to say, other matters having been carefully arranged in order for it to have the opportunity to do so. Because it takes up the right kind of space – the focused space which presents the reality it contains as self-sufficient, the phenomenon currently under scrutiny *and nothing else* – it is a conditioned truth, one deliberately shorn of the implications inextricable from whatever we perceive in the ordinary world.

The way in which art strives for clarity-by-exclusion is demonstrated vividly in all kinds of story-telling, where the choice of material to include or exclude and the order of events taking place determine the identity of what emerges as a story rather than simply a record of events taking place. Stories, whether or not they are performed as plays, simplify situations in order to increase their clarity: things stand out very clearly so that the contrast between what is obviously important for making sense of what is going on and what is not is made obvious to us. These are the things which occupy the foreground of our attention, keeping the rest out of view (or at least for the time being).

The end result, however, is not any kind of exclusion, but a more important inclusion. The intensification of the image does not diminish our awareness, but turns it in a different direction, bringing to mind things which are not immediately available to the senses. It is as if the power of a single dominant perception has the ability to anaesthetise its surrounding sensations, clearing space around itself set free from the world's furniture, almost as if it were shoving ordinary things aside to make room for extraordinary ones. Some of these are realised in terms of the image itself which expands to include us within it, in the way that a picture does when we allow ourselves the luxury to simply stand and gaze, concentrating on the picture itself, rather than any preconceived ideas we may have about it.

Once we have made contact with the image, in the action of engaging we find ourselves drawn deeper into ourselves. Far from being in any way alien to us, the world opened up by the image is one which we already know, so that we are aware of being on the threshold of a knowledge we have forgotten, a way of being ourselves which we have glimpsed but never grasped, although we have sometimes longed to do so. We still cannot grasp this profounder self, but now we have found a way of visiting it. Once this has happened we are unlikely to forget the experience.

The image leads us into and away from itself, acting as if it were a looking glass which shows us ourselves in a new way and giving us depth, so that we take on some of the significance of the image itself, reaching beyond the banal and familiar in order to be more fully alive, more authentically ourselves. And so the image makes us more real by giving us another dimension, one not yet fully explored, which holds out to us the purpose of deeper personal fulfilment. C. G. Jung calls this "individuation" and associates it with the presence within our unconscious minds of the compelling symbolic images which he calls archetypes,[51] whose presence is mediated to us in the form of all kinds of works of art. However we think of it, the experience is the same; as focus leads into revelation and the world becomes the place which, for us, it should always be.

This is something which theatre can do: not a particular kind of theatre, simply theatre itself. It is a spiritual experience, but not necessarily a religious one, although religions will certainly see it as such, just as therapists will continue to interpret it in psychological terms. In fact it is aesthetic, the art form being that which belongs to drama and cannot realistically be distinguished from it. In fact the robust nature of drama, its availability as a fundamental human experience, continues to resist attempts to reduce it to merely a form of something else. In theatrical terms the image is enough. It speaks, and the door opens for us. Whether or not we are willing to follow where the path will lead is up to us.

10

SPACE FOR CHANGE

As an Anglican nun I was called to care for thirty emotionally disturbed girls from 10 to 16 years old. Naturally there was a lot of anger and resentment due to the abuse, rejection or hurt they had suffered. We began to act out the storming of the walls of Jericho, accompanied by a Beethoven symphony. They were given permission to let out their anger in a safe way. Years later one of the girls telephoned me to say she had just heard the Jericho music on the radio.[52]

This is specifically the area of Dramatherapy, defined by an American practitioner and theorist as "the intentional and systematic use of drama/theatre processes to achieve psychological growth and change".[53] In the nun's story given above, angry adolescents were given space to express and work through their anger and be changed by this experience. In this example dramatic space is equated with the permission to allow oneself to face powerfully disruptive feelings and so find a way of reducing their pressure. Here it is anger which achieved catharsis, in other cases it would be either repressed or semi-repressed emotions – shame, guilt, jealousy, resentment; depression, meaninglessness, sexual frustration – whatever it is that reduces our sense of being at peace with ourselves and the universe.

Dramatherapy deals with personal change. Its aim is to establish a milieu in which the way we perceive the world, how we think and feel about our relationship to ourselves and it, may come to regard change as an option rather than a terrifying prospect. Being theatre-based it involves movement and gesture, exploring the connection between physical expression – embodiment – and psychological states, as this is the way in which hidden things become actual pres-

68

ences, situations which may be engaged with rather than just denied or perhaps argued away. The children in the episode described above did not merely imagine they felt the same as the triumphant Israelites; they committed their newly awakened feelings to action, marching round the city walls and blowing hard on their trumpets. The difference is an important one. Listening to a story and identifying with people in it is one thing. Allowing your own actual self to carry out actions similar to theirs is qualitatively different – and not easily forgotten.

This hands-on quality distinguishes the arts therapies from most other kinds of psychotherapy. Its success in the treatment of difficulties within human relationship is striking evidence regarding theatre's power to transform thoughts into experiences. For these children the action of walking round the walls of an imaginary city was more than a cathartic release of feelings; it was a step forward into the real world, the one we are conscious of sharing with others, a game which was real in itself and therefore about reality. The children walked in a new way and the walking itself was a way of changing. This too tells us something else which is basic to the way theatre works, particularly with regard to its use as space.

Although we tend to think of personal relationships in the abstract, we live them out in all the ways which the physical world permits. Our ways of thinking and feeling are revealed in movements towards and away from, or simply by standing still. Dramatherapy explores relationships in these terms, taking its cue from theatre, where attitudes of mind and heart show in terms of movement on stage; sometimes in the space left between one person and another or the distance between either and those playing the part of the audience (for up-staging is as effective in therapy as it is in the theatre). Dramatherapy underlines the inherent truthfulness of theatre as an indicator of psychological events which would otherwise remain hidden. This is particularly the case with improvisation, when an emotional reaction finds physical expression without the interposition of thought. These are the moments actors themselves refer to when rehearsing a role, sensing as they do that it is this precious spontaneity which lies at the heart of its authenticity.

Just as imagined action gives rise to real emotion so spontaneous reactions become bodily movement and gestures which we recognise as belonging to a world we ourselves share, and will go on doing so despite the assurances which theatre gives us that the world it is creating is an illusion. Perhaps so, we say, but the truth you are using to create it is ours, and we continue to treat it as such. In such a way, the inner space which has been brought into existence reproduces – mirrors – the play-space which was provided for us, and in which, for a couple of hours perhaps, we made a temporary dwelling place. No wonder, then, that the plays we share so often take up a more permanent residence within our memories, where they continue to influence the way in which we experience things happening in what we call the 'outside' world.

Things remembered like this were not trivial; if they had been we should have forgotten them a long time ago. They are things which have somehow left their mark. In a way which is uniquely there own, both waking and sleeping, they have changed our lives. Living within a culture which refuses to take such thing seriously, they have been our *alcheringa*,[54] the dreamtime of a spiritual pilgrimage, providing evidence of *things we know we need to know*, and steadfastly labour to resist. Resist them or not, however, they affect the choices we find ourselves making.

Perhaps it is inevitable that we struggle in this way, it being the nature of conscious awareness to discount information which it regards as unaccredited, which after all is precisely the kind of data produced by plays. There is another reason, however, which is even more important. At this deeper level theatre may well call for adjustments to be made in the way we regard ourselves and other people. Insightful experience alters both the necessity for and the possibility of real personal change, changes in the way we ourselves are people. For this reason, too, our consciousness finds ways of discounting any personal relevance which they may seem to have for us. It was, after all, only a play; and we should not be so stupid as to go looking for trouble . . .

Nevertheless, the fact remains that this is what we do. If the thought that there might be a need for us to change is so unacceptable to us, we should never have gone to the theatre in the first place. Theatre and change have always gone together: it would be hard to imagine any play at all in which the subject was not raised, but even if such plays exist they can hardly be considered as drama if no changes of any kind take place. Theatre draws its power from events significant enough to change the lives of characters within the play in ways which will arouse a response from the audience; in the absence of such events their failure to show themselves is itself a cause for distress, for without the changes which they give rise to – for which they make room – life loses its meaning. It is vitally important that Gogo and Didi should go on waiting for Godot, and therefore postpone hanging themselves "until tomorrow"; for no-one ever really knows when something unexpected, something new, might happen.[55]

Theatre longs for change, striving always to move into greater depth, deeper meaning. Those plays in which people go out of their way to avoid those things we are in the habit of describing as comedies, and the moments when they fail to do so strike us as particularly poignant and to bestow a dimension of genuine humanity which would otherwise be lacking. Again it would not be genuine theatre without such moments as it would have deprived itself of any opportunity to resonate with the human beings who comprise both actors and audience. Any description of human life must take account of our need to adapt to changing circumstances. Whether or not we are successful, we are changed by the process of living through the things which happen to us so that, looking back over our lives, we recognise the contrast between ourselves as we were and the people we are now: the dramatic contrast, in fact. Certain events, situations, relationships may stand out because of the central role which they played in creating a division into 'before' and 'after'; we may even be conscious of having been carried along in a succession of changes, not all of which were of our own making, and feel anxious because we are aware of a process which is unlikely to have finished yet.

If this is the case, theatre provides an opportunity to draw comfort from a story which has a beginning, a middle and an end, in which even situations left unfinished and hopes remaining unfulfilled are part of a wider purpose. Theatre functions along lines of circumscribed freedom. The "willing suspension of disbelief' does not involve accepting the characters and their setting as if they were real; it refers also to the recognition of a timescale arranged for a dramatic impact rather than chronological consistency. The play-space, both in its actual and metaphorical identity, makes room for such variations in time, just as it does for other divergences from normality encouraged by the 'as if' principle of drama.

Under these circumstances, too, the idea of personal change loses some of its unattractiveness having been lived out at one remove. This is not to suggest that changes occurring in the world outside the theatre will henceforth be sustained with equanimity by those personally involved in them; all the same, the relief of anxiety which is a core characteristic of theatrical experience is, as we have seen, powerful enough to remain with us whenever we look back on the changes which have happened to us in the course of our own lives, particularly if we tend to see our own life as a story about ourselves. In this way we may certainly look at our own experience of theatre as having contributed to changes of direction we are able to identify for ourselves. Theatre is a perpetual reminder of the way life changes. Seen as a part of life rather than merely a commentary on it, it gives us permission to modify, or even revolutionise, our own scenarios.

In this the giving and receiving of permission is the key factor. The children in the story recounted at the beginning of this chapter were given permission to release deep feelings of anger outside the walls of Jericho. It was the play itself and being given permission to be in it which produced this effect. The fact that it was a play made their lives more real. It gave them back to themselves in a way that one of them certainly never forgot. The exercise might be described as either drama therapy or music therapy; and in fact all the arts therapies possess this liberating quality, the ability to open doors within the mind and heart which have long remained shut. Dramatherapy in particular gives permission to move somewhere else and take more space, in this case by creating a whole new world to visit and revisit.

Dramatherapy strikingly illustrates the way in which room for movement gives the permission necessary for personal change by acting it out instead of just thinking about it. Drama becomes a place to move into in search of practical and creative ways of being human. The theatre building, its auditorium and acting area are not unfortunate necessities, there in order to support the play. They are not adjuncts of the theatre or merely its location, but its actuality, for theatre exists as somewhere to go, a place to move into. From this point of view the theatre building and everything in it is our acting area, our 'empty space', just as by the same token all space given over to drama is its own theatre. We ourselves are its guardians; we can summon it up or lay it to rest. Above all it is something we do rather than something which is done to us. A uniquely imaginative activity, it translates mental constructs into personal experiences, so that the idea of change becomes the living memory of somewhere once visited rather than simply a leap into the dark. It cannot be said to cancel out our fear of changes happening to us in our lives, but it is surely one of the factors which keep our awareness of change alive for us, so that when important changes come the shock may be less intense, less crippling, than it would have been if we had managed to keep the possibility of its occurring at arms length and concentrated in simply 'pressing on regardless'.

Theatre, the action by which we decide to allow ourselves to become involved in a play, whenever or wherever it is being presented, widens the scope of our lives by encouraging us to take the risk of reminding ourselves of things we would rather not dwell on, perhaps because they are sometimes better not thought of alone. If real change is to take place, however, they are matters which have to be faced; particularly if they are seen to relate to the prospect of having to abandon the precious security of one way of life and fall victim to the unknown. At times like this, theatre may serve the purpose of a rite of passage,[56] the transformative symbol of changes which are radical and decisive, as the audience is emotionally embraced by a moment of transformation which is not just an idea but an embodied experience – an event in life which affects other successive events and is able to change them in ways affecting their lives.

When this happens, theatre space becomes ritual ground, where the action centres upon the line dividing actors and audience. Here there is little chance of avoiding the issue: here we are brought face to face with ourselves at the point of meeting, that liminal space in which, at the most profound level of our existence, the old gives place to the new. Things which are difficult to acknowledge are very often avoided, if only because consciousness may find ways of denying the necessity to take account of them – something which, according to psychoanalysis, unconsciousness manages to do without having to think at all.

Nevertheless, theatre makes us think of these things: it does not allow us to avoid them. If avoidance contributes so powerfully to our psychological problems, then acting them out for others and ourselves is an obvious answer. To avoid them can never be to escape them; and often it is the hard psychological effort we make in order to discover ways of bypassing them which causes us so much anxiety.[57] We may not know why we are anxious, or what there really is to be anxious about, but there, in the background, the uneasiness persists. It may be that this is what Martin Heidegger identified as existential anxiety, the burden of simply being alive yet not knowing why; often however it is effort we put into in order *not* to know.[58] So far as the effect on behaviour goes, the latter is more damaging.

One of the reasons for writing this book has been the need to explore what it is that makes theatre a healing presence in our lives, resisting at the same time the pressure towards medicalisation which everything which has a therapeutic effect must undergo nowadays. To some extent this has not been difficult, because the healing which theatre mediates is not usually recognised as such by those who go to see or take part in plays. Theatre is widely acknowledged as providing a 'release of tension', a fact which is of obvious interest to psychologists (and perhaps social scientists), but apart from its specialised application under clinical or pseudo-clinical conditions in Psychodrama, Gestalt Psychotherapy and Dramatherapy, its more generalised importance for human well-being has been neglected, its identity as a vital factor in the self-awareness of individual and communities has fallen victim to the urge for specialisation, and its contribution to the quality of life in general to the current determination to gauge effectiveness solely in terms of measurable outcomes.

Of all human activities, the making and doing of plays most resists the urge to produce results which are immediately recognisable. Attempts to gauge an audience's reactions to a play before the audience has left the theatre building have generally turned out to be disappointing. People are often unready to commit themselves to examining the ways in which the play they have just been watching has affected them, and the knowledge that something of personal importance took place as a result of their involvement in it may take a little time to register. We have seen earlier how this can happen. Plays characteristically try to avoid leaving situations unresolved and questions unanswered, which is why there is usually a feeling that something has been settled for us and we don't need to discuss it further. If it was something emotional, perhaps we are unable to remember very clearly. This, too, takes time, so that we find ourselves thinking, feeling and behaving differently before we really know why we are doing it. When we do remember, however, we do not easily forget.

This, of course, is why we say that plays 'move' us. They live on in our minds and in our lives. Perhaps the reason why their effect on us is not always instantaneous is because it takes us time to accommodate them, which is what we have to do before we can start to build on them – something which always happens to plays with which we have allowed ourselves to become personally involved. One way or another, we build them into our lives. As they made room for us, we make room for them. As we have seen, this is not an easy thing to do: just as theatre's first move is to keep us at a distance, so our own initial reaction to a play which has 'got through' to us is to remind ourselves that what went on in it was not actually real. However just as the action of welcoming us into the play depends on our being, to begin with, firmly outside it, so our success in making a play part of our own personal identity requires a definite decision to ignore the rules dividing fact from fiction.

Avoidance and exclusion involve the same gesture of soul. In theatre, both are established so that engagement may take place – the meeting of selves involved in an experience of imaginative inclusion within the lives of others. Theatre-space transmits a message about exclusion while enshrining a vision of belonging.

11

THE OPEN SPACE

When actors want to say something seriously personal, they put on a funny voice. (An actor)

Side by side we sit watching what is going on in the space marked off for the actors. We are the audience and to this extent we belong together. In the same way, those in the play-space are united by being fellow members of the cast. The job of the play is to negotiate a temporary alliance between the two groups. Without the play there is very little unity. Things which belong together do so for social and economic reasons rather than personal ones. The audience's uniformity is a contrivance, a matter decided by the arrangements of seats, all of which must face the acting area. Some audience members, as of right, occupy the best seats, while others who are not able to sit down, are left standing; an arrangement which corresponds to the socio-economic divisions which exist within the play itself. There is a correspondence linking the range of circumstances and situations, personality types and individual histories in the story being enacted, to the lives of the people within the audience.

The terms of our own humanity require us to see ourselves within the context of other human beings. We are aware of an urgent need to take account of the presence of others in order to make sense of ourselves. At this basic level we are preoccupied with where we feel we 'stand' in relation to the people around us. Where do we belong? There is a temptation to answer this question in an abstract way by saying 'to the human race', and certainly this is better than not knowing how to answer it at all. Yet the question itself is not abstract; far from it. There is in all of us a primal, primitive need to know who it is that we belong *with*: otherwise how can we know who we ourselves are? To allow ourselves to become involved in theatre gives us access to a world which, although in some ways resembling ours, is in an important way radically different from it. This is not only because its reality is imaginary – for a good deal of what we regard as real outside the theatre owes its existence to imagination – but because of its way of dealing with disharmony: we turn from a humanity which is grudgingly shared with others, a jealously metered acceptance hedged about with restrictions and subdivided into classes, to one which is honest and open. The plays themselves are preoccupied with distinctions – personal, social, political – which are there to give verisimilitude, and consequently relevance to the state of affairs in the world outside. Differences inside the play call to mind ones with which we ourselves are extremely familiar.

However, here the circumstances differ significantly. Our temporary citizenship within the play is able to transform the quality of the acceptance we are willing to give to differences of this kind. What in the other world were barriers now present themselves as conflicts which will be resolved, divisions within an inclusive pattern which serves as a holding space, our own willing initiation into the play having made such a thing possible. The contradictions of which theatre is composed are there to bring home to us the short-sighted way in which we are used to thinking about our own discords, particularly those consuming our relationships with others and ourselves. By its very nature, theatre is inclusive. It explores human differences in a way which runs counter to the general assumption that people with whom we feel we have something in common are in some way superior to the rest of humanity. This is the group of people to which we belong. As Abrams, Hogg and Marques point out, "much of social life is about who we include, who we exclude and how we all feel about it".[59] This 'group-creating reflex' appears to determine our sense of belonging which, when it comes down to it, is really a case of whom we belong *among*. In theatre we open ourselves to the challenge of belonging somewhere else, somewhere different, while still having our own identity. Identity becomes the way we bestow ourselves rather than something the group has bestowed on us, although it is certainly an experience which we may want to share. The distinction between what is shared and what is my own ceases to be a problem. This space is common ground.

One way or another this space itself becomes movement: movement towards an encounter with the embodied imagination which theatre brings into the open; movement outwards from an exclusive belonging; movement into contact with experiences usually avoided and always feared; movement inwards to the undiscovered self, using space as the threshold of whatever lies beyond. This is space as liberation from exclusiveness, whose only claim on us is that we should be willing to take advantage of the offer it makes us – that we should abandon our cautiousness and step into the gap.

Theatre, then, is about overcoming exclusion by giving us the chance to enter a world totally dependent on the action of sharing: one which has no existence apart from being the embodiment of the human impulse towards mutuality. This is not to say, of course, that people involved in theatre are less selfish than the rest of humanity; but the desire to allow others to discover a joy which they themselves have known – and continue to know – acts as collateral for the generosity which they may otherwise may seem to lack. This, however, is saved for the play; actors are frequently accused of an egocentricity in their offstage lives which is nevertheless totally absent from their performances.

This, too, is something shared. The vulnerability of actors, their need to enter the safe space provided by their role within the play, chimes with that of members of the audience, who welcome the invitation to join them. They and the actors together make up a commonwealth of refuge-seekers. In this they are side by side with one another in a metaphorical sense, which is more important than the literal one. As an icon of truth-as-meeting, the space has many dimensions: of imagination, in the encounter between role and role, world and world; of human relationship in the meeting of persons; of understanding and insight as we come into contact with the depth of meaning hidden from sight by the familiar; of life in community, as individuals recognise the call for corporate action.[60]

Theatre space is an absence waiting to be filled, an offer which is asking to be taken up. It is not in itself any kind of structure, but simply an opportunity for a variety of alternative structures, an opening in the interlocked reality which holds us so tightly in its grip. As the ordinary closes in on us we turn with relief to this special place. Its availability is a sign of our own personhood and to remain unmoved by its potential is to be handicapped as human beings.

78

Where there is too intense a preoccupation with the business of protecting the self its effect is therapeutic. It cannot be made into a therapy because it already is one; which is why a consciously clinical approach is always to some extent reductionist. This is not to say that theatre ought not to contribute to psychotherapy – left to itself it can scarcely avoid doing this – but that it should not be used as an adjunct to an exclusive blueprint for psychological function.

Certainly, dramatherapists are aware of the emasculating effect of too much psychological interpretation on the power which resides in drama when it is allowed to be itself, rather than being explained away in terms of a model of human behaviour which is less direct, less immediate than the one demonstrated, the living drama of personal relationship, taking place in the space we have made for it by standing back in order to gain entrance. Theatre power is well disguised. We are amazed by the effect produced in us by something which in fact never claims to be what it seems, and in refusing to do so, encourages us to look much deeper than appearances.

We should also widen our view by showing more regard to theatre created for its own sake rather than commercial profit. Countless plays are presented for love rather than money, yet they are usually regarded, except by their audiences, as definitely inferior to professional productions simply because they are not performed by professionals. For amateurs, putting on plays is a hobby, an enjoyable way of passing time rather than part of the serious business of living. On the other hand, the growth of Theatre in Education has introduced new generations of children to a kind of theatre unknown in schools thirty years ago – an adventurous participatory drama founded in improvisation, inspired by the pioneering work of Peter Slade, Dorothy Heathcote, Gavin Bolton and others.[61]

Much of the demystification of theatre, the erosion of the belief that theatre should remain the hallowed preserve of the highly skilled practitioner, was in fact due to a professional company, Joan Littlewood's 'Theatre Workshop', which burst into London's East End in the second half of the 1960s, undermining the authority of a dynasty of theatre owners and managers whose taste had dominated the West End for decades. Joan's theatre was what it said it was: a place where materials – ideas, stories, situations; problems, solutions, disasters, unexpected breakthroughs – were worked on in order to produce something which the company could offer an audience as genuinely its own. Joan was not impressed by professionalism. Her actors were workers. In a theatre organised around the star system, her influence was powerfully democratic.

The idea of 'community theatre' owes much to Littlewood herself and theatres influenced by her such as Peter Cheeseman's theatre-in-the-round at Stoke on Trent.[62] It is no coincidence that so many schools nowadays have their own 'theatre workshops' in which plays can be put together in the tradition of the original one, with the same determination to co-operate in the sharing of insight and inspiration. Joan's vision of a theatre which would be truly democratic both in origin and effect is being realised in a way which she herself perhaps did not foresee. It turns out that after all there are other ways in which the West End can be outmanoeuvred.

Basic things about theatre are emerging, then, at grassroots level. Theatre space goes on growing as it continues to perform its age-old task of making room for us to breathe.

12

SPACE TO BE HUMAN

The conscious image of a dream.[63]

In its purest, most authentic form a play is a trauma, a dream into which we dive like seabirds, plunging below the ocean surface. Our preparation lies in the determination to engage with what awaits us. We have learned a good deal about life and death from the plays we have immersed ourselves in; but rarely, if ever, will they have been the things we were expecting. If theatre is to be seen as a technique for learning, this is the true nature of its didacticism; the demand that we abandon ourselves entirely to what is new to us so that the place we are entering is itself rather than one we have already made our own. Imagination is the breakthrough itself, not the under-standing which follows it when the smoke finally clears. All genuine artistic experience is like this, but nothing demonstrates it so clearly, so *dramatically*, as theatre.

To get the most out of this ourselves, we must leave our notebooks and theatre manuals at home. The time for script reading is over, as much with the audience as with the actors. In the position we have taken up, the space we have broken into, our scripts by themselves are no longer capable of supporting life, as only the dream can carry us where we need to go. We may think that we know where this is – we usually do – but we shall certainly be surprised by what we find and, equally importantly, by what it feels like to find it. The feeling is immediate and stays with us, as a dream does when we are awak-ened: the understanding comes later and is something we are able to work with. One way or another we relate it to our ordinary awareness of ourselves and the world as we see it.

81

Theatre deals with things which are unthinkable off-stage. It concerns itself with matters we find ourselves unable to cope with, situations we cannot handle. We avoid trying to deal with them because we are convinced that we shall fail in the attempt. The freedom which rules in an imagined reality exposes us to dangers on all sides, so that we feel naked. Theatre protects us from one reality by laying us wide open to one in which there may not be anywhere to hide. This in itself is a terrifying thought, one which makes us conscious of our own mortality, for what can we do if we see no way to turn? How can we go on existing? And yet how can we not do? Here in the theatre, dreaming is compulsory, so that in company with Hamlet we find ourselves wondering

> what dreams may come
> When we have shuffled off this mortal coil.[64]

In our case, however, it is not only the situation we are imagining which gives us pause, but also the way in which we come to imagine it in the first place in the action of exchanging worlds. This is no easy task, although the idea itself may appear harmless enough: we simply imagine a space and move into it. This, however, is not our space, but the play's; it is not our projection but a world which lies waiting for us. What we are faced with is not a transition but a transaction. Like actors hovering in the wings we get ready to jump into the arena, trying to convince ourselves that we are ready to meet what we shall find there. Perhaps we are, but is it ready for *us*?

Confrontations of such a kind have a dramatic effect, shattering the picture we cling to of a predictable world in which we recognise ourselves, producing a more or less familiar response. Recent neurological research into the psychology of trauma shows the metaphor to be analogically precise. It also demonstrates that traumatic effects may be the result of situations which are themselves imaginary. They concern the way we perceive any world which offers us an appropriate way of responding – a recognisable way. Trauma and drama represent a breakdown in expectation occurring at various levels of intensity.

Theatre creates space traumatically by breaking into the real world in a way which shocks us out of ourselves. It does so at our own invitation, but when it comes down to it the effect is the same. So why do we continue to search for opportunities to afflict ourselves in this way? Could it be that we need drama in order to survive, to reactivate the impulse to go on making sense of things by shocking us into newness? To reassure ourselves of our ability to survive the unthinkable, impossible? Theatre itself shows itself to be not simply the imitation of life but its extension: space we make to train ourselves to survive "the slings and arrows of outrageous fortune"[65] which belong to and typify our lives outside the theatre.

The way of perceiving which is characteristic of theatre is essential to us: we must have it in order to go on being ourselves. It is our dramatic awareness which sustains our personality and consequently our identity as human beings, constantly providing new *gestalten*[66] which emerge to fill the gap now left by the collapse of ways of making sense which no longer work for us.

The aversive presence of the theatre space, in extreme circumstances amounting to terror – as in stage fright – and the consequent demand to fill it, suggests that it is not the space itself which draws us but a dread of emptiness which spurs us into action in order to find a place to inhabit, a milieu for world construction. Somehow we must fill it or remain defeated by its emptiness of any perceivable meaning or significance. Theatre, however, presents this barrier as a doorway. However much it may confound us in the first instance, we look back on it entirely differently, as a way of seeing others and ourselves which is willing to take imagination seriously enough to use it as a guide for living.

Theatre gives us access to ourselves as we are. This means, of course, that it is not afraid to remind us of our fear of dying. Seen from this point of view it is a rehearsal for death – an assertion of human meaning which relieves our fear of dying by giving us space in which to experience survival. Whether or not we ourselves are afraid of death, the awareness of its inevitability gives meaning to every attempt we make to think realistically about life. Death for us is the archetypal change of scene. When we step into the space which theatre has opened for us we embrace a truth about ourselves which cries out to be acknowledged, so that in a sense we are validating the terms of our own circumscribed nature.

This is not to suggest that all plays are concerned with the conscious intention of transmitting this particular message – or even, for that matter, any message at all. The significance of theatre, any kind of theatre, lies in the dramatic event which alters our own perception of reality: not the story itself but our decision to believe in it, the contract between storyteller and audience which depends on our willingness to suspend disbelief. Whenever this happens, even in the shallowest, most patently contrived play-making, the effect can never be dismissed as simply cosmetic, as even the most meretricious theatre acts as a metaphor for living and dying if only because the world it presents provides us with the space required for our own gifts of world-creation.

How we use the space intrinsic to theatre, whether we allow it to inhibit us and send us back into ourselves or are willing to see what use we can make of it, remain largely up to us. "I don't lose myself in a part," said an actor, "I find myself in the play."[67] This certainly applies to the role we must assume as members of an audience. The play gives us the space we must have if we are to encounter ourselves; open yet private, at once personal and shared. It makes public space in crowded settings, notably those in which information about people is seen as more important than the people themselves. Wherever technological communication threatens to become more important than the meeting of persons, theatre is there to re-humanise us.

NOTES

1 Theatre Space

1 'Psychopathic Characters on the Stage', S. Freud, *Standard Edition*, Vol. 17, 2001, 305–310.

2 *Theatre and Therapy*, 2013. Walsh's book provides a useful overview of ways in which therapy has used theatrical approaches.

3 In *Aristotle's Theory of Poetry and Fine Art* (1951) S. H. Butcher provides a penetrating analysis of Aristotle's text and its application to Greek classical tragedy.

4 N. Evreinov (1927); V. Iljine (1910); L. Moreno (1924); F. Perls, R. F. Hefferline, P. Goodman (1973); S. Jennings (1990); P. Jones (2007).

5 Peter Brook (1968), *The Empty Space*, p. 9.

6 D. W. Winnicott (1971), *Playing and Reality*.

7 The phrase 'the willing suspension of disbelief' was originally applied to poetry by S. T. Coleridge in 1817. Nowadays it is almost always used in connection with theatre, however. (See Grainger, 2010.)

8 See *Man and His Symbols*, ed. C. G. Jung, 1964, pp. 206–7.

9 'Tell all the truth but tell it slant': Emily Dickinson, *The Complete Poems* (edited by T. H. Johnson), 1975. Poem 1129, p. 506.

2 Play-Space

10 Shakespeare, *Henry V*, The Prologue.

11 Shakespeare, *Hamlet*, Act II sc. 2.

12 Christopher Marlowe, *Dr Faustus*, sc. VI.

13 See R. Grainger, *Nine Ways the Theatre Affects our Lives*, Edwin Mellen Press, 2013, Ch. 2.

14 Personal communication from an actor.

15 R. Grainger, *op. cit.*, Ch. 2.

16 On the subject of liminality, 'fear of thresholds', see Victor Turner, *The Ritual Process*, 1974; also Mircea Eliade, 1958, 1965.

17 Personal communication.

3 Angry Space

18 S. H. Butcher, 1951, pp. 346*ff*.

19 See note 7.

20 Antonin Artaud, *The Theatre and Its Double* (trans. Victor Corti), 1970, pp. 62, 63.

21 The quotation comes from *Shadows of Ecstasy* by Charles Williams, 1933.

22 *Psychology and Alchemy*, 1944 (*Collected Works of C. G. Jung*, Vol. 12, p. 160f.

23 Charles Williams, *op. cit.*, p. 188.

24 See Martin Buber, *Between Man and Man*, 1961, *passim*. Martin Buber is the philosopher who has contributed most to our understanding of personal relationship.

4 Remembered Space

25 The phrase is associated with Jean-Paul Sartre, for whom it represented the action of free human choice, which "presupposes that there is a plurality of possibilities, and in choosing one of these [people] realise that it has value only because it is chosen." It is in this that its "truth" lies. J-P. Sartre, *Existentialism and Humanism*, 2007, p. 36.

26 Michel Foucault, *Language Counter-Memory and Practice*, 1977, p. 182.

27 Martin Buber, *Pointing the Way*, 1957, p. 66.

28 Michel Foucault, *op. cit.*, 1977.

5 Occupied Space

29 R. Landy, *Persona and Performance*, 1993.

30 Erving Goffman, *The Presentation of Self in Ordinary Life*, 1971; *Forms of Talk*, 1981. See also R. Grainger, *Suspending Disbelief*, 2010.

31 This information was supplied by a former member of Peter Hall's company.

32 Miller Mair, 'The Community of Self', in *Perspectives in Personal Construct Theory*, 1977. ed. D. Bannister.

33 See *Building a Character*, Constantin Stanislavski, 1950, *passim*.

34 *Henry V*, Prologue to Act I.

6 Private Space

35 Frederick Langbridge, *A Cluster of Quiet Thoughts*, 1896.

36 This is the line as it is usually quoted. The original version by Gertrude Stein reads: "Rose is a rose, is a rose is a rose" ('Sacred Emily', 1913).

37 George A. Kelly, *The Psychology of Personal Constructs*, 1991.

38 See J. Willett, *The Theatre of Bertolt Brecht*, 1959: 'grund-gestus' is at once gesture and gist, attitude and point" (p. 173).

39 By "integration", Jung means "the struggle for the wholeness of the personality . . . at once a task, a goal and the highest good to which man can attain on earth" (Jolande Jacobi, 1942, p. 102).

40 See note 32.

7 Functional Space

41 Lewis Carroll, *The Hunting of the Snark*, 1870, line 8.
42 This is a subject which I have treated at some length elsewhere (Grainger, 1988, 1990, 1995, 2009).
43 Martin Buber, *I and Thou*, 1966, p. 41.
44 Percy Bysshe Shelley, 'Song', in *Posthumous Poems*, 1824.
45 Martin Buber, *op. cit.*, p. 3.

8 Space to Manoeuvre

46 See Mircea Eliade, *Rites and Symbols of Initiation*, 1958.
47 Barbara Pym, *An Academic Question*, 1987, p. 163.
48 See R. Grainger, *Nine Ways Theatre Affects Our Lives*, 2013, p. 71*ff*.

9 Space as Depth

49 August Strindberg, *A Dream Play*, adapted by Ingmar Bergman, 1973.
50 'Whispers of Immortality' in T. S. Eliot, *Collected Poems*, 1936.
51 'Individuation' is self-realisation in the sense of personal fulfilment: "Over against the polymorphism of the primitive's instinctual nature there stands the regulating principle of individuation . . . together they form a pair of opposites. This opposition is the expression, and perhaps also the basis of the tension we call psychic energy." ('On Psychic Energy', in *Collected Works of C.G. Jung*, Vol. 8).

10 Space for Change

52 Jean Naylor, personal communication, 2013.
53 Robert Emunah, quoted in Phil Jones, *Drama as Therapy*, 2007, p. 8.
54 See James G. Cowan, *The Aborigine Tradition*, 1992.
55 Samuel Beckett, *Waiting for Godot*, in *The Complete Dramatic Works*, 1986. See also R. Grainger, *The Uses of Chaos*, 2010, ch. 5.
56 The phrase 'rite of passage' is from Arnold van Gennep. See *The Rites of Passage* (trans. M.B. Vizedom and G.L. Caffee), 1960.
57 See Perl's description of the way we double our anxiety by being anxious about being anxious. (F.S. Perls, R.F. Hefferline and P. Goodman, *Gestalt Therapy*, 1973, p. 500.)
58 See Martin Heidegger, *Introduction to Metaphysics*, 2000, p. 21.

11 The Open Space

59 *The Social Psychology of Inclusion and Exclusion*, ed. D. Abrams, J. Marques and M.A. Hogg, 2004, p. 2.
60 See, for example, Augusto Boal's 'Theatre of the Oppressed' (1979).
61 Peter Slade, *Child Drama*, 1954; Gavin Bolton, *Towards a Theory of Drama in Education*, 1979.

62 Peter Cheeseman was Director of the Victoria Theatre in Stoke on Trent in the 1960s. He was responsible, along with his casts, for a ground-breaking series of 'documentaries' illustrating the life of the local community.

12 Space to be Human

63 J. C. Trewin, *The Gay Twenties*, Macdonald, 1958, p. 17.

64 *Hamlet*, Act III sc. 1.

65 *Hamlet*, Act III sc. 1.

66 Ian Hunter defines 'gestalt' as "a configuration, pattern or organised whole, with qualities different from those of its components", (in Bullock and Stallybrass, 1977).

67 Personal communication. (The actor prefers to remain anonymous.)

BIBLIOGRAPHY

Abrams, D., J. Marques, and M. A. Hogg (Eds.) (2004). *The social psychology of inclusion and exclusion*. Hove: Psychology Press.

Artaud, A. (1970). *The theatre and its double: essays*. London: Calder & Boyars. Translated from the French by Victor Corti.

Beckett, S. (1986). *The complete dramatic works*. London: Faber.

Boal, A. (1979). *Theatre of the oppressed*. London: Pluto. Translation by Charles A and Maria-Odilia Leal McBride of *Teatro de Oprimido*.

Bolton, G. M. (1979). *Towards a theory of drama in education*. London: Longman.

Brook, P. (1968). *The empty space*. London: MacGibbon & Kee.

Buber, M. (1957). *Pointing the way: collected essays*. London: Routledge & Kegan Paul. Translated from the German by Maurice Friedman.

Buber, M. (1958). *I and thou*. Edinburgh: T & T Clark. Translated by Ronald Gregor Smith.

Buber, M. (1961). *Between man and man*. London: Collins. Translated by Ronald Gregor Smith.

Bullock, A. and O. Stallybrass (Eds.) (1977). *The Fontana dictionary of modern thought*. London: Fontana.

Butcher, S. H. (1951). *Aristotle's theory of poetry and fine art: with a critical text and a translation of the Poetics* (Fourth ed.). New York: Dover.

Carroll, L. (1876). *The hunting of the snark: an agony in eight fits*. London: Macmillan.

Cowan, J. G. (1992). *The elements of the Aborigine tradition*. Shaftesbury: Element.

Dickinson, E. (1970). *The complete poems: edited by Thomas H. Johnson*. London: Faber and Faber.

Eliade, M. (1958). *Patterns in comparative religion*. London: Sheed and Ward. Translation by Rosemary Sheed of (1949) *Traité d'histoire des religions*, Paris: Payot.

Eliade, M. (1965). *Rites and symbols of initiation: the mysteries of birth and rebirth, etc.* New York: Harper & Row. Translation by Willard R. Trask of *Naissances mystiques. Essai sur quelques types d'initiation, etc.*; published 1958 as *Birth and rebirth: the religious meanings of initiation in human culture . . .*

Eliot, T. S. (1963). *Collected poems 1909–1962*. London: Faber & Faber.

Evreinov, N. N. (1927). *The theatre in life*. London: G G Harrap & Co. Edited and translated by Alexander I. Nazaroff.

Foucault, M. (1977). *Language counter-memory practice: selected essays and interviews*.

Ithaca, NY/Oxford: Cornell University Press/Blackwell. Translated from the French by Donald F. Bouchard and Sherry Simon.

Freud, S. (1953). Psychopathic characters on the stage. In *The standard edition of the complete psychological works of Sigmund Freud: SE 7:305*, pp. 305–310. London: Hogarth and the Institute of Psycho-Analysis. Translation from the German of *Psychopathische Personen auf der Bühne* under the general editorship of James Strachey, in collaboration with Anna Freud, assisted by Alix Strachey and Alan Tyson.

Goffman, E. (1971). *The presentation of self in everyday life.* Harmondsworth: Penguin.

Goffman, E. (1981). *Forms of talk.* Oxford: Blackwell.

Grainger, R. (1988). *The message of the rite.* Cambridge: Lutterworth.

Grainger, R. (1990). *Drama and healing.* London: Jessica Kingsley.

Grainger, R. (1995). *The glass of heaven: the faith of the dramatherapist.* London: Jessica Kingsley.

Grainger, R. (2009). *The drama of the rite: worship, liturgy and theatre performance.* Brighton: Sussex Academic.

Grainger, R. (2010). *Suspending disbelief: theatre as context for sharing.* Brighton: Sussex Academic.

Grainger, R. (2010). *The uses of chaos.* Bern: Peter Lang.

Grainger, R. (2013). *Nine ways the theatre affects our lives: dramas of transformation.* Lewiston, NY: Edwin Mellen Press.

Heidegger, M. (2000). *Introduction to metaphysics.* New Haven, CT: Yale University Press. Translation of *Einführung in die Metaphysik* by Gregory Fried and Richard Polt.

Jacobi, J. (1942). *The psychology of C. G. Jung: an introduction with illustrations.* London: Kegan Paul. Translated by K. W. Bash.

Jennings, S. (1990). *Dramatherapy with families, groups and individuals: waiting in the wings.* London: Jessica Kingsley.

Jones, P. (2007). *Drama as therapy: theory, practice and research* (Second ed.). London: Routledge.

Jung, C. G. and M.-L. von Franz (Eds.) (1964). *Man and his symbols.* London: Aldus.

Kelly, G. A. (1991). *The psychology of personal constructs: Vol. 1. A theory of personality Vol. 2. Clinical diagnosis and psychotherapy.* London: Routledge.

Landy, R. J. (1993). *Persona and performance: the meaning of role in drama, therapy, and everyday life.* London: Jessica Kingsley.

Langbridge, F. (1896). *A cluster of quiet thoughts.* London: Religious Tract Society.

Mair, J. M. M. (1977). The community of self. In D. Bannister (Ed.), *New perspectives in personal construct theory*, pp. 125–149. London: Academic Press.

Moreno, J. L. (1977). *Psychodrama: Volume 1* (Fourth ed.). Beacon, NY: Beacon House.

Perls, F. S., R. F. Hefferline, and P. Goodman (1973). *Gestalt therapy.* Harmondsworth: Penguin.

Pym, B. (1987). *An academic question.* London: Grafton.

Read, H., M. Fordham, and G. Adler (Eds.) (1953). *The collected works of Carl Gustav*

Jung: vol. 12. Psychology and alchemy. London: Routledge & Kegan Paul.

Read, H., M. Fordham, and G. Adler (Eds.) (1960). *The collected works of Carl Gustav Jung: vol. 8, The structure and dynamics of the psyche.* London: Routledge & Kegan Paul.

Sartre, J.-P. (2007). *Existentialism and humanism.* London: Methuen. Translation from the Frend and introduction by Philip Mairet.

Shelley, P. B. (1824). *Posthumous poems.* London: J. & H. L. Hunt. Edited by Mary Wollstonecraft Shelley.

Slade, P. (1954). *Child drama.* London: University of London Press.

Stanislavsky, K. S. (1950). *Building a character.* London: Reinhardt & Evans. Translated from the Russian by Elizabeth Reynolds Hapgood.

Strindberg, A. (1972). *A dream play: adapted by Ingmar Bergman.* London: Secker and Warburg. Introduced and translated from the Swedish by Michael Meyer.

Trewin, J. C. (1958). *The gay twenties: a decade of the theatre.* London: Macdonald.

Turner, V. W. (1969). *The ritual process: structure and anti-structure.* London: Routledge & Kegan Paul.

Van Gennep, A. (1960). *The rites of passage.* London: Routledge & Kegan Paul. Translation by Monika B. Vizedom and Gabrielle L. Caffee of (1908) *Les rites de passage* Paris: Nourry.

Walsh, F. (2012). *Theatre and therapy.* Basingstoke: Palgrave Macmillan.

Willett, J. (1959). *The theatre of Bertolt Brecht: a study from eight aspects.* London: Methuen & Co.

Williams, C. (1933). *Shadows of ecstasy: a novel.* London: Victor Gollancz.

Winnicott, D. W. (1971). *Playing and reality.* London: Tavistock.

INDEX